OPEN SPACES, CITY PLACES

OPEN SPACES, CITY PLACES

Contemporary Writers on the Changing Southwest

Edited by
JUDY NOLTE TEMPLE

THE UNIVERSITY OF ARIZONA PRESS
Tucson & London

The University of Arizona Press
Copyright © 1994
The Arizona Board of Regents
All rights reserved
⊗ This book is printed on acid-free, archival-quality paper.
Manufactured in the United States of America
99 98 97 96 95 94   6 5 4 3 2 1
Library of Congress Cataloging-in-Publication Data
Open spaces, city places : contemporary writers on the changing
Southwest / edited by Judy Nolte Temple.
    p.   cm.
   Includes bibliographical references.
   ISBN 0-8165-1165-9 (cl : acid-free paper). —
   ISBN 0-8165-1440-2 (pb : acid-free paper)
   1. American literature—Southwestern States—History and
criticism—Theory, etc.   2. Southwestern States—Intellectual life—
20th century.   3. Southwestern States—In literature.
4. Southwestern States—Civilization.   5. City and town life—In
literature.   6. Country life—In literature.   I. Temple, Judy Nolte,
1948–   .
PS277.O6   1994
814'.540803279—dc20   93-35926
                                              CIP

British Cataloguing-in-Publication Data
A catalogue record for this book is available from the British Library.

Rudolfo Anaya's essay was published in a somewhat different form as "The Myth of
Quetzalcoatl in a Contemporary Setting: Mythical Dimensions/Political Reality" in
Western American Literature 23 (November 1988): 195–200, and is reprinted here
with permission of the journal. Rolando Hinojosa-Smith's essay originally appeared
in *The Texas Literary Tradition*, edited by J. W. Lee, D. Graham, and W. T.
Pilkington (Austin: University of Texas Press, 1983) and is reprinted here with
permission of the publisher.

CONTENTS

Contents

ACKNOWLEDGMENTS

The idea for the Open Spaces, City Places Conference, from which this book arose, grew out of endless debates with Charles Bowden. Kathy Dannreuther of Tucson Public Library helped me write—and rewrite—the National Endowment for the Humanities grant proposal that made the conference possible. Thomas Phelps, our NEH program officer, provided intellectual guidance and well-timed morale boosts. He predicted that we could produce a book from the conference without additional NEH support, and the commitment of the essayists proved he was right.

Special thanks go to the Tucson Public Library staff, whose efforts made the December 1987 conference a success. Mac McClenahan, the project assistant, ensured that the conference came off without a hitch. Rotha Trainor transcribed and typed manuscripts, interpreting the squiggly marks and tape recordings that became a book. Persistent folk at the University of Arizona Press brought this project to a close; they are Joanne O'Hare, senior editor, and Robyn Forkos, editorial assistant.

Open Spaces, City Places is dedicated to the memory of Reyner Banham, desert enthusiast, who did not live to see this book. Reyner and his wife, Mary, attended the conference during a respite in his bout with cancer. Their wit and love warmed us.

INTRODUCTION

> Location is the ground conductor of all currents of emotion
> and belief and moral conviction that charge out from the
> story in its course. These charges need the warm hard earth
> underfoot. . . . One place comprehended can make us
> understand other places better. Sense of place gives
> equilibrium; extended, it is sense of direction too.
>
> Eudora Welty
> *The Eye of the Story*

Eudora Welty's wise advice is a difficult challenge for the writer in the
modern Southwest. What if he is Native American and sees the remembered earth of his homeland dismembered as its young people leave for
alluring cities? What if she is Hispanic, living in a small barrio home,
hungrily listening to her family's stories about the freedom of the
rancho, forever lost? Or what if the writer grew up in a slow-paced
Southwestern town that within his life span has quadrupled its size to
become a Sunbelt metropolis where the warm, hard earth is paved over?
What is the role of the writer in the changing Southwest?

Most writers of serious Southwestern literature have taken one of
three thematic routes in their search for continuity amid such rapid
change. One tactic is to draw on collective past traditions, to create literature steeped in mythic experience. Writers such as N. Scott Momaday, Rudolfo Anaya, Leslie Marmon Silko, and Frank Waters have
created memorable stories of contemporary characters whose lives are
salvaged by an infusion of ancient wisdom. Other writers have chosen
to turn their attention to the past and present wondrous open spaces of
the Southwest: the late Edward Abbey, J. P. S. Brown, and Ann
Zwinger. A third route, used on occasion by Abbey, John Nichols,
Leslie Marmon Silko, and Larry McMurtry, attacks the development of
the Southwest head-on, humor barely hiding the rage. In *Lonesome*

Dove, McMurtry's most popular and acclaimed novel, the anti-urban theme is set in the spacious old West so magnetic to readers. Aging Texas Ranger Augustus confides to his friend that he hates the very West he helped settle:

> The dern people are making towns everywhere. It's our fault, you know. . . . If I'd wanted civilization I'd stayed in Tennessee and wrote poetry for a living. Me and you done our work too well. We killed off most of the people that made this country interesting to begin with.

This, in my opinion, is the dilemma facing modern Southwestern writers. Their very presence in the region helps populate it; their writing about its open spaces draws others to the Southwest, where newcomers love the desert to death by building homes and paving roads. The writers love the open spaces, caressing them with words, yet seek the intellectual and cultural stimulus of the city. They increasingly find themselves in two worlds: they write about the land while they live in the city. Only in today's Southwest do so many write that which they do not live.

It can be argued that Southwestern writers are merely creating what sells. And in a region of rapacious growth, the image of open spaces is most popular. The easiest thing for lovers of the Southwest to do in response to quantum change is to bury their heads in the sands of an imagined endless desert rather than read about the urban areas they inhabit. They feast their eyes on landscape calendars as traffic chokes their neighborhoods. They read novels set in the wilderness of Monument Valley rather than confront the urban wilderness downtown. They peruse popular histories of the Anglo cowboy West while lounging in houseboats afloat on Lake Powell instead of reading about the damming of the Colorado River and water burial of Glen Canyon and ten thousand Anasazi Indian sites. Historian Ann Douglas has shown that sentimentalized icons in nineteenth-century America, such as children, religion, and motherhood, were actually undergoing great devaluation. It is as if, by sugar-coating that which is dying, we hope to forestall its demise and freeze it within our memories as it disappears before our eyes. The state of Southwestern writing and readership may be the symptom of such a death.

The disparity between the urban life of Southwestern writers and readers—and the nonurban/anti-urban setting of their most popular works—lends both a tension and a sense of unreality to much of the region's writing. While much of contemporary American literature focuses on critical realism, Southwestern literature dwells primarily on the mythic, the spacious—the past. Those popular books that do deal with Sunbelt cities lambaste urban blight while literature celebrating city life often is fostered only by small presses.

Open Spaces, City Places attempts to address this dissonance, place it in the context of American literary history, and explore some of the little-known literature and fresh voices that are emerging from today's Southwestern cities. A number of concerned writers have contributed to this collection; their approaches to the topic are as diverse as the Southwest. Often the writers have more questions than answers. This collection is itself motivated by a series of questions:

- Is the Southwest truly modern, or is it a unique bi-temporal region containing within its boundaries both Indian hogans and urban high rises?

- Exactly what are the open spaces of the modern Southwest? Are they figments of the imagination, pristine primitive areas protected by/for man, playgrounds for the physically fit, tomorrow's ranchette home-sites?

- Is literature about the open landscape its eulogy, or a healthy rebellion by writers in defiance of encroaching urbanization? Can literature that speaks on behalf of nature make a difference?

- Can there be a universal literature in a region that houses a strongly defined cultural triptych of Anglo, Hispanic, and Indian voices?

- Is fiction an outmoded genre for dealing with modern Southwestern experiences? Do other literary forms, such as new journalism and binary/bilingual amalgamated writing, better fit this Brave New World?

- What is the role of a mythic Southwestern spaciousness in the American psyche? John C. Van Dyke argued at the turn of the century that the deserts are the last breathing spaces of this country. Must Southwestern artists, then, like Sisyphus, endlessly bear the mythic burden for the entire country?

- Is anti-urbanism the last surviving frontier value? Can Southwesterners in a changing region define themselves only as *not* Eastern or

Western urbanites? If Los Angeles didn't exist for Southwesterners to ridicule, would they have to invent it?

Open Spaces, City Places is divided into four sections, each containing overviews of selected Southwestern literature as well as personal responses to the open spaces/city places dichotomy. Several of the writers and scholars argue that the opposition is a false one, that placed in the context of American intellectual history, ambivalence toward urbanization is deep within the American grain. Hawthorne captured this tension in *The Scarlet Letter*: Hester lures her lover onto the forest path, arguing, "Backwards to the settlement. . . . Yes, but onward too! Deeper it goes, into the wilderness. . . . There thou art free."

The first section, "Open Spaces, City Places," contains three essays by writers who inhabit Southwestern cities yet carry the land deep within their hearts and histories. The writers represent three distinct literary approaches to the Southwest: essayist/historian Stewart Udall, journalist Charles Bowden, novelist Rudolfo Anaya. Each writer has witnessed phenomenal change in the region of his birth, each despairs at the Southwest's future, and each presents a different response to the urbanization of the region. The fourth essay, by Leo Marx, places this struggle to maintain a pastoral vision amid urbanization within the context of American letters. Marx argues that Southwestern literature is a case study of pastoralism and sees a forbidding future for a region and a nation so enamored by the idea of wilderness.

The second section, "Open Spaces," contains three essays about the appeal of nature to American writers and readers. Frederick Turner and Peter Wild argue that this appeal is a false one, based on an anthropomorphic sentimentalization of wilderness. Ann Zwinger provides an account of her own journey into nature—and nature writing. She presents an alternative perspective toward open spaces as home rather than as an abstract idea. All three essayists contrast the intellectualized vision of nature as a panacea with the raw power of Western spaces. They suggest that not confronting nature realistically dooms true wilderness.

The third section, "Writing Along the Edges," focuses on literature about life on the border—the border between cities and open spaces, between cultures, between past and present, between nations. In reality, this is the region most Southwesterners inhabit, a place where change stirs the emotions, where cultures mix, clash, enrich. Four essayists de-scribe the uneasiness and ultimate creativity that come from change in the Southwest.

Luci Tapahonso lives in the diverse worlds of urban academia and the Navajo reservation, worlds that fuel her poetry. Don Graham explodes the myth of the landscape that urban Texans consume. Rolando Hinojosa-Smith recalls a far different Texas, one of border people making a new life while remembering the old in their literature. Finally, Tom Miller surveys literature of the ultimate region of Southwestern ambivalence, the Mexico-U.S. border. This essay takes the topic of cities to the geographical and cultural limit by studying what creative writers have done when confronted by border culture. While this section oscillates between love and hate for Southwestern cities, it provides insight into the cultural discomfort that can lead to creativity.

The final section of the book, "City Places," celebrates the rich life in the urban Sunbelt. Patricia Preciado Martin finds Chicano neighborhoods to be rich gardens full of experiences and lessons from the old ones. It is the rapidly changing cityscape, Martin suggests, that lends an urgency and care to her task of collecting stories about her culture. Lawrence Clark Powell and the late Leland Sonnichsen, respected Southwestern men of letters, end with the wisdom that age and much reading provide. They see no dire conflict between the region's open spaces and city places. Powell suggests there is a vitality in cities that fosters art; Sonnichsen, that the resolution has existed in the Southwest all along.

I hope that the mixture of personal and scholarly essays will enrich those who care about the Southwest. The cacophony of so many voices speaking from such diverse viewpoints is the sign of a lively debate and of concern. This collection is dedicated to the idea that writers who love the Southwest should have as much of a voice in the fate of the fastest-growing region in America as do planners and politicians. We do well to heed their words.

—Judy Nolte Temple

OPEN SPACES, CITY PLACES

Development in low foothills on Sunrise Drive near Sabino Canyon in Tucson. (Photograph © Jack W. Dykinga)

STEWART L. UDALL

Creative Freshets in the Arid Southwest

The best way to approach a collection of essays based on a conference is to treat it as a kind of potlatch to which thinkers bring ideas, insights, and biases, then have an exchange. I will express my own convictions and my own biases, but as far as the big questions that are raised by the juxtaposition "open spaces, city places," I'm not sure any of us have the answers.

I am essentially anti-city. I was asked in 1962, when I was talking about the environment of the nation, what did I think the optimum population was for the United States? I said about one hundred million people, roughly what it was in 1900. And I think, as far as Arizona is concerned, the optimum is about where we were in 1916; and the same way with Tucson. This, of course, is nostalgic, it's reactionary, even sentimental. I plead guilty to all those accusations.

I also have a bias for small towns and hope that small towns will be sustainable in the next century. There's a wonderful line in *Fiddler on the Roof*. Remember Tevye, the wonderful protagonist of that musical play? He was a small towner. He said, "There is one thing that you should remember about Anatevka. In Anatevka everyone knew who he was and what God expected of him." Well, that's a pretty good description, not just of a Jewish town in eastern Europe but of every small town, at least the kind of a small town where I grew up. Even neighborhoods, good neighborhoods, distinctive neighborhoods in large cities, offer a special experience that is very precious for humanity.

And look close by here. At Taos, or at a city named Wagon Mound,

New Mexico. One of the people who grew up in Wagon Mound was Fray Angélico Chávez, a Franciscan priest who, to me, is the most interesting person in New Mexico. He was a young poet whom T. S. Eliot praised in the 1920s. His masterwork, *My Penitente Land*, a kind of autobiography, a meditation on Spanish New Mexico, is one of the finest books that has been written about the Southwest.

Something I leave with you as an old-timer's message is Don't be afraid of myths. For authors and writers, the myths and mythical world are as important as the real world. Don't be afraid of being romantic. Don't be afraid of having a love affair with the land or with a place.

Can we preserve regional literature? I think we can. I still believe that there can be Southwestern writers. I think there is a rich field here to be plowed and harvested. Let's give some encouragement to those artists and writers in our part of the country who are trying to prove the case for our region.

Robert Frost once said to a group of writers at Breadloaf in Vermont, "There ought to be in everything you write some sign that you come from almost anywhere." In his case we know that the stamp of New England north of Boston was deeply imprinted on his work. And that is what he was saying to us—that place is not just geography; that place is, as he said later, a region of the mind. I believe a reaction to a New England environment ought to be different from, say, a response to a New Mexico or Tucson or Ventura environment. Not only our place of growing up in our formative years is important; the land, the natural world where we grew up, leaves a stamp on us.

I am in my early seventies, and my childhood years were spent in a small town. This is where my impressions of life began. I didn't know, of course, that in my childhood years Willa Cather was in Santa Fe and was working on *Death Comes to the Archbishop*. I didn't know who D. H. Lawrence was. But I know what some boys read in this region in the 1920s. We read Zane Grey and Ernest Thompson Seton and Harold Bell Wright of Tucson and such authors. That's where our part of the country was in terms of its literary interests and its production of literature.

I do not doubt that what we call the Southwest has undergone major changes. I first really saw our broad region in the late 1930s. You didn't travel much during the Great Depression. Most of my travel was as a member of the University of Arizona basketball team; we went to El Paso and Las Cruces and Albuquerque and other places. And I lament the loss of that Southwest. It's a matter of sorrow to me to talk about the environments of our cities then. Tucson had a population of about thirty-five thousand, and Phoenix wasn't much larger. All of these cities—Tucson, Phoenix, Albuquerque, El Paso, Santa Fe—had a strong Spanish flavor in those days. It was a very strong influence in so many different ways. Today all of the cities have lost it, in my view, except Santa Fe. Santa Fe has lost some but is still a distinctive city, for it has retained part of the ambience and culture that distinguished it in the 1930s.

Tucson still calls itself the Old Pueblo. But where is the Old Pueblo? I was reminded by some preservationist friends that the site of the true Old Pueblo, of the old original forts, is being readied for "development." Where is our interest in our past—in the preservation of the cultural differences that distinguish our region? A friend came to Phoenix not long ago, and said to me, "Show me old Phoenix." And I didn't know where to begin. I live in a part of old Phoenix, and there are a few byways and places I can take a visitor, but Phoenix is trying to be like Dallas and Houston and the Southwest's other look-alike skyscraper cities. And Tucson is following in lockstep, I fear.

Another thing that bothers me is that cowboys in Arizona are an endangered species. When I was a kid, Arizona was a state of ranches. Now they are going, going, gone. I shed a tear every time I read about it. And many of our distinctive small towns are being disfigured. My own small town of St. Johns is now an energy town. Phoenix and Tucson used to be health resorts, and now they're in the top five in terms of some kinds of air pollution. Clare Booth Luce said that when she first came to Phoenix in the 1930s, and drove through the city, she had a feeling that she was passing through a garden. If you remember the Phoenix of that time, there were a lot of citrus orchards and flower gardens. She said, "The garden is gone." And it is.

One of the paramount environmental issues today in Arizona is that although we have some of the most productive agricultural acreage in the world, we are going to convert all our farmland into another Los Angeles.

There has been some discussion among intellectuals in this country whether we have reached a stage where there can no longer be regional writers. Some seem to doubt that we can have authentic regional writers in our era as a TV "global village." I hope they are wrong. I think one of the wonderful things about our country is its regional diversity. Once there was a Yankee culture in New England, and in other areas of the United States there were important cultural and regional differences. There were differences in architecture, and differences in language and customs. Now our culture is supposedly being homogenized, and we are supposed to applaud. Well, I hope some folks fight against this homogenization. The great homogenizer, of course, is television, because it brings us all together. It makes us, they say, a national village in which we think the same way and have the same outlook on life and the same values and imagination. I hope we resist this trend, because life is richer when there is diversity, when there are differences, where there are arguments, when there is striving. The "Open Spaces, City Places" theme helps us focus on some of these differences.

What are the factors that influence art? What do writers and artists call upon in terms of their total experience as they seek to interpret what they see and what they live? What forms the natural and social matrix of their lives?

In any society we can have only a few who become the towering artists, but there is also an art in the populace at large that is very important: not only in terms of appreciation of the great works of art but also because there is another level, it seems to me, in terms of the meaning of the everyday lives of everyday people. Where each individual is concerned, the interpretation of what is true and what is beautiful is very important. And so whether we are artists or ordinary people, the environment that we live in is what nurtures us: the man-made environment of the city, God's environment in the natural world, and the social environment, the interaction between human beings, between cultures. I believe this is one of the areas where we are richest in our region: the splendid diversity of cultures that we have here. There is in the Southwest an ambience, and above all, we need to sustain it.

One thing that influences the sensibilities of people in the Southwest is that it is arid. It has vast landscapes; it has exceptional natural beauty; and it has a cultural diversity that confers an exceptional cultural beauty. We have in this part of the world, for example, the richest and most varied Indian cultures in the United States, we also have a Hispanic culture that is very beautiful and very diverse, and it gives us something very special. The Southwest is endowed with both a natural environment and a man-made environment that are singular. This should be reflected in our culture and in our writing. I think we have as one of our great assets in the Southwest not only an extraordinary natural beauty but also an extraordinary opportunity to let nature infiltrate our minds and influence our outlook on life.

I'd like to share some ideas offered by one of our finest Western writers, Wallace Stegner. Stegner was maybe the only recent writer who had won the Pulitzer Prize for both history and fiction. This is what he wrote in *The American West as Living Space*:

> I have lived in the West, many parts of it, for the best part of seventy-seven years. I have found stories and novels in it, have studied its history and written some of it, have tried to know its landscapes and understand its people, have loved and lamented it, and sometimes rejected its most "western" opinions and prejudices, and pretty consistently despised its most powerful politicians and the general trend of their politics.
>
> If there is such a thing as being conditioned by climate and geography, and I think there is, it is the West that has conditioned me. It has the forms and lights and colors that I respond to in nature and in art. If there is a western speech, I speak it; if there is a western character or personality, I am some variant of it; if there is a western culture in the small-c, anthropological sense, I have not escaped it. It has to have shaped me. I may even have contributed to it in minor ways, for culture is a pyramid to which each of us brings a stone.[1]

If Wally Stegner were here, I would say that perhaps we have a better chance in the Southwest of maintaining the distinctiveness that he described in his fine essay.

This sense of a place was expressed wonderfully in a poem by Archibald MacLeish. Of the events that I was involved with when I was secretary of interior in the 1960s, this is one I will always remember. I had gotten acquainted with Carl Sandburg's family through his daughter, and when he died in the early summer of 1967, it occurred to me that we should do as the French do when their great literary figures die, and have a national memorial service in a famous public place. Carl Sandburg had written a poem about what he wanted done when he died. It was very, very simple: ring a bell and play certain songs.

And they carried out his wish down in North Carolina.

But I thought we should have a national memorial service on the steps of the Lincoln Memorial for Carl Sandburg, Abraham Lincoln's biographer. The family liked the concept, and we did it one Sunday

afternoon in September 1967. The main part of the program involved
readings by two poets from Illinois, Archibald MacLeish and Mark Van
Doren. They read his poetry and they talked about him; Archibald
MacLeish had written a poem for the occasion. It stresses the importance of the regional distinctions that gather around the themes of this
collection of essays. He called the poem he read that afternoon "Where
a Poet's From."

WHERE A POET'S FROM

                    Where he's born?
Settles? Where the papers claim him?
Carl Sandburg, born in Illinois,
died in Flat Rock, Carolina, in Chicago famous—

where was Sandburg from? Chicago?
People knew where Frost was from
in spite of San Francisco—from New England.
What town or what proud country knew this other coming?

He lived around: he lived in Kansas,
Chicago on the Old West Side,
Michigan, Nebraska—in Wisconsin.
Where was Carl from in the Carolinas when he died?

His tongue might tell: he talked "Peoria"—
O as in Oh or Low, the way
the railroad trainmen on the Illinois
called it in those cool reverberating stations.

His sound might say: he said "Missouri"—
a stumbled M and an S and an OO
long as a night freight off across the prairie
asking the moon for answers and the sound goes through
and through.

Where was Sandburg from, old poet,
dead in Carolina in this great repute?

"Peoria," he said, "Missouri," the neglected names
that now, because his mouth has spoken them, are
beautiful.[2]

Where *is* a writer from? This is a wonderful question we should ask
when we read the work of any author.

I have one quarrel with the idea that our last open spaces are going
to disappear. This may be the best hope of all, at least in terms of what
I have referred to as the natural legacy we enjoy in this part of the
world. Not long ago, a realtor put up a sign on the highway from
Williams to the Grand Canyon that read, "Only fifteen percent of Arizona can be bought or sold." It's true. Think of that for a moment.
What this sign says is that most of the land in Arizona is owned by all
of us as a common heritage.

We have in Arizona, for example, a larger total number of national
parks and national monuments and national historic sites than any
other state. In fact, the most beautiful, the most scenic area in the whole
world is the Colorado Plateau that stretches from the Grand Canyon to
Monument Valley to Moab, Utah. There are more national parks in
that region than in any other part of the United States. It is an extraordinary area. And all of us own it as a common glory.

As a matter of fact, Tucson is part of a distinctive natural environment. You can fill the Tucson bowl with high rises and houses, but this
city is unique among the large cities in the United States. This is a city
surrounded on two sides by detached sections of the magnificent
Saguaro National Monument. Within a mile is a designated wilderness,
Pusch Ridge. And you have national forests surrounding this bowl on
the north and east and south. Tucson has a spacious outdoor legacy—
and all of us own it!

If you want to take a small boy and walk out of Tucson, you can go
into the mountains and you won't see No Trespassing signs. You own
it. It is part of your heritage. As long as this public ownership prevails,
there will be a special environment here.

And never forget that twenty-seven percent of the land in the state of
Arizona is Indian-owned, the largest percentage of any state in the
union. And these are lands the Indians will hold and preserve, or develop, as they see fit.

Finally, I think we in the Southwest must begin at last to recognize the full glory of our Spanish heritage, and the pivotal role Hispanics have played in our history. I believe we may very well have, in the late 1990s, a Hispanic Hemingway. Some of the young writers who are coming along show great promise.

I want to end by quoting from the final passage of my book, *To the Inland Empire: Coronado and Our Spanish Legacy*. I got so fascinated studying the Spanish part of our history that when I finished, I felt I knew these young men, these first Europeans who came into this part of the New World and discovered the Grand Canyon and buffalo and the greater Southwest. Here is the eulogy I wrote to celebrate the deeds of these young Europeans:

. . . it demeans the quest of the conquistadores to portray them as mere actors in a gold rush. Many undoubtedly hoped for easy wealth, but there was also a passion to achieve what Shakespeare called "the bubble reputation." Spaniards were anxious to leave an illustrious legacy for their families, so the prospect of winning personal glory was surely on the minds of some of the soldiers.

. . . We must not forget that the faint-hearted stayed home, and that those who chose to embark on long voyages, or to go as adventurers to *tierra incognita* were bold individuals, mentally prepared to risk life itself on the ventures they undertook.

It was the Italian sailor/scribe Antonio Pigafetta who wrote that when he signed on as a member of Ferdinand Magellan's fateful crew, he was ". . . prompted by a craving for experience and glory." Experience and excitement were intoxicating inducements to young men living cramped lives in Spain's austere, small towns.

. . . But returning to Don Francisco Vazquez de Coronado and his friends, one wonders how they reacted when, their entrada only a memory, they sat in the shade the long years afterwards. Did they regret that those who knew little of their odyssey or what they accomplished regarded their adventure as a failure? Were they haunted by memories of the Bigotes, and the buffalo and the Grand Canyon and the high clean silences of mesas and plains where they wandered in their youth?

Sometimes poets supply answers to such questions. It is our good fortune that one of our finest bards, the late Archibald MacLeish, became fascinated with the lives of the conquistadores and wrote an epic about their adventures and memories.

The protagonist MacLeish chose for his poem was, of course, Bernal Diaz, who wrote his "true history" autobiography to correct misinterpretations made by Gómara, the professor in Spain who had composed a pompous history about the conquest of Mexico. Here, as one answer to our speculations about the autumn thoughts of aging conquistadores, is the summation Archibald MacLeish put into the mouth of Bernal Diaz as he sat down to write about "that which I myself have seen and the fighting . . .":

I am an ignorant old sick man: blind with the Shadow of death on my face and my hands to lead me: And he [Professor Gómara], not ignorant—not sick—

                              but I
Fought in those battles! These were my own deeds!
These names he writes of mouthing them as a man would
Names in Herodotus—dead in their wars to read—

These were my friends: these my dead companions:
I: Bernal Diaz: called Castillo:
Called in the time of my first fights El Galan:

I here in the turn of the day in the feel of
Darkness too come now: moving my chair with the change:
Thinking too much these times how the doves would wheel at

Evening over my youth and the air's strangeness:
Thinking to much of my old town of Medina
And the Spanish dust and the true rain:

I: poor: blind in the sun: I have seen
With these eyes those battles: I saw Montezuma
I saw the armies of Mexico marching the leaning

Wind in their garments: the painted faces: the plumes
Blown in the light air: I saw that city:
I walked at night on those stones: in the shadowy rooms

I have heard the chink of my heel and the bats twittering
I: poor as I am: I was young in that country:
These words were my life: these letters written

Cold on the page with the spilt ink and the shun of the
Stubborn thumb: these marks at my fingers

These are the shape of my own life . . .

and I hunted the

Unknown birds in the West with their beautiful wings![3]

NOTES

1. Wallace Stegner, *The American West as Living Space* (Ann Arbor: University of Michigan Press, 1987).

2. Archibald MacLeish, *New and Collected Poems, 1917–1982* (Boston: Houghton Mifflin, 1985), 479–480.

3. Stewart L. Udall, *To the Inland Empire: Coronado and Our Spanish Legacy* (Garden City, N.Y.: Doubleday, 1987), 212–215.

CHARLES BOWDEN

Dead Minds from Live Places

A desert breeze blew round me. I thought of that ruined castle in distant Syria which Lawrence had visited. The Arabs believed that it had been built by a prince of the border as a desert palace for his queen, and declared that its clay had been kneaded with the juice of flowers. Lawrence was taken by his guides from room to crumbling room. Sniffing like dogs, they said, "This is jasmine, this violet, this rose"; but at last one of them had called, "come and smell the very sweetest smell of all," and had led him to a gaping window where the empty wind of the desert went throbbing past. "This," they told him, "is the best: it has no taste."

Wilfred Thesiger
Arabian Sands

She calls and says two things concern her: the Yaqui arrowhead her father had given her, and a necklace of rare stone. She does not talk long, it is not her phone. Twenty years before, she'd been a calm voice, long legs, cat eyes, a woman strumming the guitar as we sat around drinking and getting stoned and wondering how you carved a life out of a cow town in the desert. We considered jazz a possible antidote: Ornette Coleman, Pharaoh Sanders, Bird, Miles. Or folk, or blues. Her fingers were very slender then, her hair long. We were certain we all must leave, that much we knew. I stumbled into her again in San Francisco, where there was a regular colony of Tucson expatriates. The skirt was short, black, and leather. The music was free every Sunday in a finger of Golden Gate Park that knifed through the Haight.

I go out to see her. The institution sulks under the dry Tucson sky. They take away my keys—sharp edges—and we must sit in the room with the group. One old woman with dyed black hair and a Walkman

talks up a storm about the bad craziness of modern life, her limbs claw-
ing in toward her as she walls herself off from life. An old man smokes
and stares ahead. She tells me with a smile that you know you've been
put in the good ward when they trust you with a lit cigarette.

My friend says, "You don't know what horror is until you have been
insane. Like being frozen in time."

The hair is short now, the figure still slender. She plays the banjo
rather than guitar.

She wonders about the arrowhead, it is very precious to her. She has
given it to an Indian boy, hoping it will prompt something important
within him. But she wonders about its future. Chances are the lockup
will be only seventy-two hours. They have no space in the ward. She
had stopped taking her pills and life crashed over in enormous waves,
and she went down in the undertow. These things happen.

We laugh a lot about the last two decades. She tells me she was driving down the freeway and meditated on her automobile, focused how
the mass of metal under the hood would stay free and cool and all the
parts would work together in harmony. It turned out meditation was
not enough, the machine needed a little oil. When it froze up, the cop
came along. She had once complained loudly to a cop and gotten off.
She tried this tactic again. She got the three-day lockup in the loony bin.

When I read about the Southwest, my friend does not often make the
book. But this should hardly matter to me. Practically nothing I have
seen or done or felt ever makes the book. That is apparently not what
literature is now about. And that is why I avoid reading it whenever
possible.

Two of the best modern novels about the real Southwest are in tech-
nicolor. One of them has a story line something like this (that is, when
one carefully deconstructs the text): a habitual convenience store robber
marries a lady cop and they want a kid but can't have one, so they steal
one from a rich furniture store owner. Complications follow, two escaped convicts drop into the plot, a convenience store gets robbed, a
bank gets robbed, the kid gets kidnapped again, and a biker-from-hell
takes up the trail for a possible bounty. In the end, the kid is returned to
its natural parents, and the two protagonists contemplate moving to
Utah.

The second example of modern fictional techniques takes place in

Prescott, Arizona: a rodeo performer returns to his hometown, finds out that his brother is bulldozing the home ranch and slicing it up into ranchettes and subdivisions, that his dad is about to hit the road for prospecting in Australia, that the bull he must ride in the local rodeo might bust his chops, that the woman he picks up in a local bar is a big city number but lots of fun over the short haul, and that you can't go home again, unless you can stomach home after it has all gone to hell.

The first novel is a comedy called *Raising Arizona*, and the second one is Sam Peckinpah's *Junior Bonner*; both of them are movies made to make lots of money and help folks kill time on rainy days. And they tell us more about how we now live in the Southwest and what it feels, looks, and tastes like than the garbage truck loads of books regularly ejected from the region's creative writing departments. They do this for several reasons. They are relentlessly urban, as is the region. They mix the Southwest's great natural beauty with its abundant human ugliness. They take it for granted that it is a place of false values, fast-buck artists, mental defectives, and that it is being degraded and perhaps destroyed. They recognize *the fact* of Southwestern life; we build nothing that matches our terrain. This would not seem to be much of an accomplishment except for the literary dementia that characterizes the books I come across. I live in a region where almost all of the literature ignores the simple fact that for one hundred years this region has been urban, rock-hard urban.

Let us waste no time with the obvious argument that art can concern itself with anything and that it is boorish to lay down strictures about its appropriate subject matter. Of course, this is true. What I want to consider is why so little art in the Southwest considers that we live in booming instant cities full of tanned bodies, vigorous crime, healthy doses of narcotics, and endless streets of ugly, mass-produced houses. I'll put it another way: What would you think if everyone writing and painting and taking photographs in the New York City of 1910 was cranking out stuff like Washington Irving's *Legend of Sleepy Hollow*? That is pretty much what I see happening in the American Southwest.

Lying about the West in general and the Southwest in particular has been an American cottage industry for over a century. The very term "the Western" is synonymous with fraud, sentimentality, and flim-flam.

In an odd way, we have gotten ourselves into the same position as Henry James when he made his famous lament about America being barren ground for a real literature, that whining, disgusting, simpering litany that ran

> . . . items of high civilization, as it exists in other countries, which are absent from the texture of American life. . . . No sovereign, no court, no personal loyalty, no aristocracy, no church, no clergy, no army, no diplomatic service, no country gentlemen, no palaces, no castles, nor manors, nor old country-houses, nor parsonages, nor thatched cottages, nor ivied ruins; no cathedrals, nor abbeys, nor Norman churches; no great Universities, nor public schools—no Oxford, nor Eton, nor Harrow; no literature, no novels, no museums, no pictures, no political society, no sporting class—no Epsom nor Ascot!

In the Southwest, we have dodged the fact of our raw, instant civilization by doting on strands of Native American culture, worshiping conquistadores or long-dead clerics, having wet dreams about former psychotics who were handy with guns, dipping into visions of vanished peoples who left comely stone ruins. It is a lot easier to find a good book about Navajos or gunfighters than about real estate developers. Which ones do you think have done more to change the face of this land?

I think we should face a few rude facts. We have created a civilization in the modern deserts, one barely a century old, that is so attractive and powerful in the eyes of our fellow citizens, that they flock to it despite shrinking water supplies, low wages, and darkening skies. Yet we cannot seem to face our acts in our imaginative literature or grapple with them in our histories. We say practically nothing about such matters. We live in exploding cities and fall mute when confronted with what we see. And the fortunate appearance of a *Milagro Beanfield War* or a *Monkey Wrench Gang* hardly undercuts this claim.

The best of all writing in the Southwest today appears in newspapers and magazines. I'd rather read *The Texas Monthly* than most of the drivel produced by our universities. One of the curiosities about modern scholarship is that it stops abruptly when it gets near the present. Just look at the titles and how they pick an end date conveniently remote from the bustle of our own world. You might claim an exception for political science, but these groups of decision makers (a term that I guess covers everything from contract killers to elected officials) can write about anything they want, since no one can possibly understand what they are saying and nobody reads them.

Normally, arguments about the unreality of literature and scholarship have spun off charges that such works ignore issues of race or sex or class. But the Southwest has carved out a truly unique body of work, one that largely ignores everything that currently exists and dotes upon worlds that never existed.

I buy a couple of thick, dull books a week and wade through some of the most boring material ever scribbled in my diligent effort to get some understanding of what in the hell is happening around me. I can't get no satisfaction. And then, because of my work, I keep bumping into the grubby habits of modern life and wondering why they are not the grist of our novels, histories, paintings, and photographs.

He lives through the telephone. It is 10 a.m., and the calls flood in from around the city, the talk never stops, and the talk is deals. He is a hundred years deep into Tucson, his family roots twine back into conquistadores, and he spends his every waking moment selling the ground out from under his past, present, and future.

A few months back his fee from ramming a real estate deal through the city government ran to eighty thousand dollars. He summered on the Coast off that one. Now he is busy refilling his coffers. There is this ground west of town that always floods and is worthless, but now, with the arrival of the Central Arizona Project, he and the boys have noticed the big canal will act like a buffer dam; they see millions in the virgin tracts. He scurries about, lining up options here and options there, the conversations punctuated with jokes, laughter, and darts of numbers. He is the wildlife of my desert now.

He is about to go hunting at an exclusive lodge in Sonora and shows me his Parker shotgun. I am moved by the beauty and craftsmanship of the weapon and struck by his eye for quality.

The phone rings, he disappears into another conversation. A shopping center here, a higher density there. The face smiles into the receiver, the voice rises and falls, barks and wheedles, teases and snaps. He is alive on the phone. I do not have to hear the party on the other end—the message is always the same: Get this through, let's have a done deal. He is a man who always has new jokes to tell you, a running part of his amusement with life. He is laughing now and asks, "Did you hear the one about the guy whose wife was acting funny? Well, he takes her to the doctor and the doc looks her over and says, 'She's got either

Alzheimers or AIDS.' The husband says, 'Christ, what should I do?' And the doc says, 'Well, on your way home, stop the car about five miles from the house and kick her out. Then go home and wait. If she shows up in a few hours, don't fuck her.'"

This is the story we all apologize for and then laugh at.

I sit on the sofa as he works the phone, call by call. Somewhere out in the smog of the city, men wait with cement trucks, bulldozers, stakes, pipes, bricks, wires, blueprints. They wait for these calls to finish, for the deal to be a done deal. And then they will move.

There is never enough money, nor will there ever be enough. The expenses can be surprising—tickets and a suite at the Superbowl. Special golf tournaments in distant states. New cars, additions on the house, dinners at serious restaurants with limited menus. The house on the beach, safe from the breath of a desert summer.

I sip my coffee from a clear glass cup; he looks over at me, beaming as his patter pours into the receiver. I like him. He knows who he is. He is at work, and the work seems never to end.

> "No, there is nothing about the desert that is romantic or beautiful. I have my garden, where the water flows bountifully from my well, I have electricity which gives me a radio and air conditioner. I can sit at my ease and drink Coca-Cola. You are made to go into the desert."[1]

The history of the Southwest for the past century has been one of taking. Cheap and easy resources have beckoned successive waves of vandals—cattle barons looting the grass; Eastern capital ripping minerals out of the soil; the military seizing large patches of earth for playing with the toys of war; federally subsidized agriculture growing redundant crops, gutting aquifers, and slowly stilling the ground with salt; American culture confining and browbeating Native American views of the world. And now real estate fortunes based on slicing land into various configurations and peddling off the remains.

With the exception of religious communities such as the grand experiment of Utah, it is a history peopled by men and women almost empty of any vision larger than money. It has two great traits. One is frenzy and rapid action as instant cities rise up without easy motives. And second is great visibility. This last point is seldom remarked upon, but I think it is very important: in the Southwest the arid landscape makes the work of human beings incredibly visible and naked. What passes for growth and progress in other regions, here makes people wince.

Very little of merit is written about this taking. The Western in its various guises is almost always a bogus, stilted genre much like Japanese samurai movies—there are wonderful exceptions, such as Larry Mc-Murtry's *Lonesome Dove*, a book so fine it doubtless will take years for it to muster a reputation with serious critics and scholars. The histories of agriculture are weary tales of triumph in the desert; the histories of government bureaucracies are like kept women, pleasant but predictable fans of their patrons. As for the cities and towns, there have been thousands of studies, each neatly independent of the other and isolate, like river-smoothed gravel strung along a library shelf, each stone waiting mute, polished, and pointless—forever.

History should help us understand why we are the way we are by examining the way we were. In the Southwest, there is a chasm between the Indian wars and the present that is bridged only by the technical monographs of tenure-seeking employees of state degree factories, a bridge frail and not worth crossing.

The stairway is lined with framed letters from politicians who have benefited from the man's advice. He is forty, successful in the advertising business, and now ready to flex his muscles in other arenas, such as elections. Once he worked with the poor in New York City. Once he wrote poetry and won prestigious prizes. He is dressed perfectly, the shirt sewn onto his body, the trousers without a wrinkle, the shoes polished and never marred.

He tells me he likes his creature comforts, and for that reason decided to leave poetry for selling. On the wall is a poster: POVERTY SUCKS. He is disappointed in people who oppose the future, who naysay the boom of the Sunbelt. They are not realistic. He figures things will be fine for fifteen or maybe twenty years. Then, he is not sure he will want to live here.

I listen with my mind, intent on making a record. I do not judge. There is no point. Some things are, some things exist. His desk is spotless, and out the window the grubby city sprawls and mutates into new forms of money. Sometimes I wish to curse this conversation and men in his business. I want to denounce the fact that I am mired in a civilization that lives by killing land, an act that will surely, in the end, kill the civilization itself. But I do not understand. And the hard part is not the understanding. Greed is an easy attitude to comprehend. It is the flutter of my own appetites when the talk spins on about yachts, summer at the beach, tennis at the club, automobiles that move swiftly from zero to sixty and then keep going toward one-sixty. I want to strike out, but all I see is myself. My face looks warped, like the image in the circus fun house.

The voice is a model of control, a slow-speed voice so that everyone must alter to his rhythm, to his control. Now he faces a decision. Two people wish to be governor of the state. No one wants either, but they both want it. He must pick between their two campaigns: Which one should he run? I ask him how he will decide. He says he will go to work for a million dollars.

And then we talk about tennis.

In the Southwest the missed opportunities are enormous. We have witnessed, and are continuing to witness, one of the largest peaceful migrations of modern times. This movement of people and money is occurring in a landscape that offers perfect viewing, in a time when our instruments of recording—film, tape, still photographs—are superb, cheap, and widely available. And we have the advantage of the past, of knowing the unanswered questions about the genesis of the great nineteenth-century efforts at new human conglomerations like Chicago, Kansas City, San Francisco, Los Angeles, and finding answers right before our eyes. But we do not.

Surely our descendants will wonder about their ancestors—yes, we must not only live, but then die and wear the dreary tag of ancestors—who plunked millions down into areas of little water, meager fossil fuels, and low-density biomasses, onto ground used recklessly for testing nuclear weapons or stuffing away toxic wastes, into regions where the last surviving homelands of non-Europeans continue into the present and where an incredible migration of Hispanics is slowly and relentlessly taking place. They will wonder why we did it, how we did it, what it felt like, what it meant. And I guarantee you that, based on our present achievements in analysis and historical and imaginative writing, they will find their best understanding in books based on streetwise reporting or films made in Hollywood for entertainment and quick profits. Would you go to scholarship to understand that thin line between the United States and Mexico? Or would you pick up Alan Weisman and Jay Dusard's *La Frontera*, carve out time for a viewing of Jack Nicholson in *The Border*?

Brawley, California, is a leaden cloak that hangs off the shoulders of the residents. I slowly grasp the fact: a century of American energy, hundreds of millions of dollars, giant canals, big dams, and the busy federal bureaucrats have created a zone of boredom, hay fields, unemployment, and resignation. And then called the mess the Imperial Valley.

The sun is slowly starting to set as Gloria goes to work. She is twenty-three and leans against a car fender, slurping a huge Pepsi. A pickup rolls up, she pours into the open window, there are quick words but no agreement, the truck speeds away. On her wrist is a six-inch scar—"I got in a gang fight when I was fourteen. I won. The operation cost six thousand dollars." She is heavy from her recent pregnancy, a girl born in February, and her arms and face are studded with tattoos: blue dots on her chin and both wrists, and on one shoulder the name Rebecca for her mother and her child. On the other shoulder is BROLE, the name local Hispanics use for Brawley. She says she kicked heroin and cocaine a few months back. I do not believe her. The words tumble out quickly and in a flat tone, as if she were racing through her morning rosary.

She comes from a family of nine kids; her dad drives a tractor, an uncle is a bartender across the street. The face radiates intelligence and ruin, and I am drawn to her. Flesh hangs off her soft frame, but the eyes cut like a knife. We do not speak of the business. Her words are very tired. I want to know what she has learned but I never will. The price of such knowledge is all over her body.

I am drawn to her. We talk, a car pulls up with two Anglo kids, blond, the radio blaring. They beckon, she ambles over, leans in to discuss possible business, then straightens up and walks back. They laugh and race away. She says nothing of her brief errand. I stand with Gloria in the 110-degree Brawley street as dusk seeps across the town.

"The cops?" her flat, yet soft, voice asks. "They don't bother much, they're all rookies now and scared of the people. I'm just going to stay here and raise the kid in this heat. I left in '79 for the Job Corps, that's where I got these tattoos—I wish I could get rid of them—and I spent the time in San Diego. I came back here."

San Diego, the name spins my mind. I am strolling on a downtown street, the neon sign says Golden West Hotel. I look into the lobby, a long, bare strip of small white tiles leading up to the forbidding desk that is festooned with big signs warning guests of all the devilish things they must not do in their rooms. Two women about thirty sit on a hard wood bench, their legs crossed. They look up into my eyes and consider if I mean business. San Diego has always been where Americans go to escape America and find they have run out of country. It is a trap where you can sit in the sun or play racquetball or raise flowers. You can do anything you want except matter.

We cannot face the West we found or the West we sacked. It is all in the photographs. I am walking through the Museum of Photographic Art in San Diego. The exhibit offers two centuries, the nineteenth and our own. Cameras eat the terrain. The artists are going to make the flesh and blood simple for us. It is all there in black and white. Outside the walls, Balboa Park is full of lush growth, flowers, and bird song. In here with the white walls and clean frames, the world is mainly prints of mountains and deserts and big rocks and huge trees. Vistas drip down the walls, rectangles cage the terrain into form and light and shadow. The planet was created in those six arduous days only to model for a lens. The dry ground feels the knife, winces, and is anointed art. People drift by, talking softly as if in a church, clutching the show's handout of information like a trail guide. The West of the photographs is the natural wonder there for the taking. The taking itself is seldom viewed as worth the talents of a photographer. We have raised up generations of them, all blasting away at Yosemite or the Rockies or Death Valley or the silhouette of a saguaro. The focus is fine, the contrast perfect, the sharp teeth of our world almost always absent. No highways, no bulldozers, no beer cans, no men, no women, no children, no life. Whenever I walk in the desert, I think of the photographs because they seem magical—they express nothing that I see or feel or think as the hundreds of miles move through my body. They are the West of the artists.

One year of San Diego was enough for Gloria. "I like working outdoors more than indoors," she continues. "I don't really have any problems, I just take my days as they come. Get cut up? Naw, I'm from around there. The block? I'd rather have them knock it down. It's not right for kids growing up to see what happens around here. I don't want my kid to go through what I've gone through. I don't know what

I want to do. I don't want to tell people what I really do. Tell them I make $240 a month on welfare. How much is that an hour? You figure it out. You can divide."

As a young boy I was fascinated with William Cody, and as a man I continue to be. Buffalo Bill represents the best and worst elements of Americans confronting the West. Cody is the lover who rapes the object of his love and then lives by selling pornographic movies of his lustier moments. We can find his face anytime we care to look in the mirror.

It is important, though difficult, to remember that Cody was a real person who impressed his contemporaries. He really did work for the Pony Express and make record-breaking rides, he really did slaughter large numbers of bison, he really did kill Indians in close combat. He was, by the rough standards of the young West, a man of mark. And he really did become a cartoon of himself through dime novels, Broadway plays, and Wild West extravaganzas. He should not be that strange to a generation that professes to worship the fragile desert once it has been provided with all the energy and power of twentieth-century gadgets, a herd of nature lovers armed with 4x4 vehicles and cameras, a group whose sensibility drives them to live in large modern cities and who decorate their walls with objects of prehistoric design or with photographs empty of a modern clue, even a road or a power line. I have a friend who recently sold a photograph of a proposed wilderness and was appalled when a careful examination of the image revealed a telephone line snaking through the saguaros. Had he known, he would have shot the picture so that this fact of who we are and how we live would have been carefully edited out by the lens.

I do not think we will ever have a literature or body of work that will matter, either to ourselves or to those who come after us, until we cease such acts. I do not know what this literature will be like. Except that it will be characterized by an effort to understand rather than obsession with ignoring.

In the Southwest we face a rare opportunity. We can view something akin in scale to nation building occurring right before our eyes. We live in a time when the memory of the taking is still alive, and when the fact of the raping is our daily bread. We live in a place where the ecological verities that seem vague in moister, more resource-rich regions are plain and measurable. On a planet where a future of overpopulation and declining standards of living because of past and present looting is inevitable. We cannot miss this fact. Because we have so little, and what we experience is happening so fast, we can see through the glass clearly. We are the provincials who live on the cutting edge of a larger culture.

What we do about this fact will be on our heads. And what we do about this fact will be our only achievement, either in cement or stone or on paper, in film, in music, and ultimately in memory. Whoever we are, this activity will be all we will eventually be.

Perhaps Plato was right, and ideas are the only reality. If so, we're likely to bore the hell out of everyone who comes down the pike after us.

> Sometimes the words just don't come, because there is something holding them back. It don't do no good to just make something up. You can't say it if you don't feel it right. The words don't come. If you just say something to sound good, you might hurt somebody, or it might come back and hit you hard. You have to sit there and wait for it to come right out of your own body. Maybe it don't come. Then you know something is really wrong inside you. You can't force it out. You just have to try to live right and then maybe it will come out of you some other time.[2]

NOTES

1. William Polk and William Mares, *Passing Brave* (New York: Alfred A. Knopf, 1973).

2. Washoe speaker of the Native American Church (Peyote), early 1950s.

BIBLIOGRAPHY

Begin with the works of Edward Abbey, J. P. S. Brown, Ken Kesey, John Nichols. Feed on the daily newspapers, monthly magazines. Be hopeful about photographs—eventually they will escape the prison of polarized lenses and glowing chollas. Attend movies before poetry readings. Listen to the singers in saloons. Always remember Abbey's definition of reason: "knowledge in the arms of love." Then go out into the streets and let it happen to you.

RUDOLFO ANAYA

Mythical Dimensions / Political Reality

Many of us who live in the Southwest have developed a mythical dimension that enables us to relate to the land and its people. This dimension keeps us close to the land and its history. We value the indigenous myths that evolved on this continent. Now the tremendous economic changes that came with the Sunbelt boom that began in the 1960s have not only altered the landscape, they have altered the way people relate to the land and each other, and there is a danger of losing this dimension. Many of us are asking what happens when we lose our mythic relationship to the earth and allow only the political and economic forces to guide our way of life.

I take much of my identity from the values and tribal ways of the old Nuevo Mexicanos, from their legends and myths and from the earth, which they held sacred. In this essay I turn my attention to the processes of world politics and economics that are altering the Southwest so radically. The growth of the Sunbelt has altered our perception of our landscape: the personal, the environmental, and the mythic. The old communities, the tribes of the Southwest, have been scattered, and they have lost much of their power. If we do not take action now, that creative force of the people which has nourished us for centuries may be swept aside.

Our future is at stake. We who value the earth as a creative force must renew our faith in the values of the old communities, the ceremonies of relationship, the dances and fiestas, the harmony in our way of life, and the mythic force we can tap to create beauty and peace. We must speak out clearly against the political and economic processes whose only goal is material gain.

It is the individual's relationship to the tribe and one's response to the elements and the cosmos that give shape to our inner consciousness. These relationships create meaning. They have shaped the Indian and Hispano Southwest, just as they have shaped part of the Anglo reality and myth. But the old communal relationships are changing as the new urban environments change our land. The diaspora that began in the 1940s has continued, the once-stable villages and pueblos are emptied to create a marginalized people in the ghettos of the new urban centers.

Many of us no longer live in the landscape our parents knew. We no longer enjoy that direct relationship with nature which nurtured them. The Southwest has slowly changed, becoming an urban environment. We no longer live in the basic harmony that can exist between humanity and the earth. A new and materialistic order has become paramount in the land, and we have little control over this intrusion. By and large, the land that nurtured us is now in the hands of world markets and politics.

True, some of our neighbors survive in mountain villages and pueblos, on ranches and reservations. These folk remain an historical link to our mythic dimension. They keep the values and communal relationships of our grandparents, and they struggle against the destructive development that characterized the past.

Urban Sunbelt population growth; renewed attention to the oil, gas, and mining industries; the construction of air bases and weapons laboratories; and a high-tech boom with its dream of a new economy are some of the elements of the politicizing process that our generation has seen become reality in the Southwest. The full force of that change has been felt in our generation as the New York and world money markets gained control over and exploited the resources of this land.

The signs of the web of the political world are all around us. Visit any of the large cities of the Southwest and you see unchecked growth, a plundering of land and water, and a lack of attention to the old traditional communities. Immense social disparity has been created overnight. We have lost control over our land. The crucial questions for us are, Have we been defeated? Have we let go of our old values?

Because I am interested in and understand the power of literature, I have to ask what this means to writers from the Southwest. For some it means a retreat into formula: the cowboy-and-Indian story is still being churned out. Some writers armed with computers simply make that formula longer and more ponderous to read. For others the retreat means moving out of the city to the suburbs or if possible to the villages or the mountains. The Indian and Chicano way of life is idealized as the refusal to deal with the new, engulfing economic and political reality grows. Some draw closer to the Indian and Hispanic communities, to the old tribes of the land, seeking spiritual warmth from, and reconciliation with, these earth people. Others create new tribal centers: Zen centers, mosques, and monasteries in the desert, hippie communes. Some writers just drink and quarrel more, subconsciously surrendering to the old Western movie plot in their withdrawal.

In my lifetime I have seen this tremendous change come over the land. Most of my contemporaries and I have left our Hispanic communities and became urban dwellers. The people, the earth, the water of the river and of the *acequias* (the irrigation canals), and the spiritual views of the tribal communities that once nurtured me are almost gone. The ball game has changed, and it is appropriate to use the ball game metaphor, because the original game of *la pelota* in Mesoamerican history has a spiritual orientation, a deep meaning for the tribe. Now it is played for profit. In our most common ceremonies and rituals we see the change, we see the new view of the West.

Politicizing the Southwest has meant corralling people in the city. Reckless developers take the land for the false promise of the easy life where homogenized goods and services can be delivered. Work in one's cornfield has become work for wages, wages which can never keep up with ever-spiraling taxation. The pueblo plaza or village post office where the community once gathered to conduct both business and ceremony has become chaotic urban sprawl. The center has been lost.

What does this mean to me—I who have now lived longer in the city than in the rural landscape of my grandparents, I who have seen this drastic change come over the land?

When I was writing *Bless Me, Ultima* in the early 1960s, I was still tied to the people and the earth of the Pecos River Valley, the small town of Santa Rosa, the villages of Puerto de Luna and Pastura. The mythic element infuses that novel because it is a reflection of the world I knew. Now the West has lost its natural state, and development after development sprawls across once-empty desert. Growth and change are inevitable, but that which is guided only by a material goal is a corrosive element that has insidiously spread its influence over the land and the people. How can I write and not reflect this process?

Who has taken charge of our lives? We are now informed by television, the daily dose of news, the homogeneous school system, and other communication media that are in the hands of the power manipulators. Many ancient ceremonies and dances are still intact along the Rio Grande, but even the people who sustain these ceremonies are affected by the bingo parlors and quick cash. My city is hostage to those who control the flow of the river, and the quality of that water will continue to be affected by the chemical and nuclear waste it washes away. This reality must affect our writings.

The Chicanos, Indians, and old Anglos who worked the land are now a labor force to serve the industries that the world economic and political system imposes on us. The time is disharmonious; no wonder we gather together to discuss the changing landscape, and the changing humanscape. We know we have been manipulated, and in the resulting change we feel we have lost something important.

Our people have been lulled into believing that every person can get a piece of the action. We set up bingo games as we pray for rain, and we train our children to take care of tourists even as they forget to care for the old ones. We begin to see the elemental landscape as a resource to be bought and sold. We do not dream the old dreams, we do not contemplate the gods, and less and less do we stand in front of the cosmos in humility. We begin to believe that we can change the very nature of things, and so we leave old connections behind, we forget the sacred places and become part of the new reality—a world reality tied to nerve centers in New York, Tokyo, London, and Hong Kong.

The old patterns of daily life are forgotten. The cyclical sense of time that once provided historical continuity and spiritual harmony is replaced by atomic beeps. The clock on the wall now marks the ceremonies we attend, ceremonies that have to do with the order of world politics. It is no wonder we feel we are being watched, our responses recorded. We are being used, and eventually we will be discarded.

But there is hope. The sensitive writer can still create meaningful forms that can be shared with the reader who is hungry for a mythic sensibility. We still have the materials and beliefs of our grandparents to work into poetry and fiction. Reflection in our writings need not become mired in paranoia. The old relationships of the mythic West need not be reduced to a formula. Technology may serve people; it need not be the new god. If we flee to the old communities in search of contact with the elemental landscape and a more harmonious view of things, we can return from that visit more committed to engaging the political process. We can still use the old myths of this hemisphere to shed light on our contemporary problems.

We, the writers, can still salvage elements of beauty for the future. We can help preserve the legends and myths of our land to rekindle the spirit of the old relationships. We can encourage the power of creativity that takes its strength from the elemental and mythic landscapes. The problems we face are not new: prior generations of Mesoamerica dealt with many of the same problems.

In exploring the legend of Quetzalcoatl while writing *The Lord of the Dawn,* I was astounded at the close parallels between the world of the ancient Toltecs of Tula and our own time. Then, as now, men of peace and understanding struggled against the militaristic and materialistic instincts of the society. Both the historical king and the deity known as Quetzalcoatl came to the Toltecs to bring learning in the arts, agriculture, and spiritual thought. Under the benign rule of Quetzalcoatl, the Toltecs prospered. But much of their prosperity was taken by the warrior class to conduct war on the neighboring tribes. Toltec civilization rose to its classic apex, then fell.

In the end, Quetzalcoatl was banished from Tula. The materialists of the society, who waged war and conducted business only for profit, had their way. The deity who brought art, wisdom, and learning was banished, and the Toltec civilization fell. The influence of Quetzalcoatl was later felt in the civilizations of the Aztecs and Mayas, for every society seeks truth and the correct way to live.

Even now, the story of the Toltecs and Quetzalcoatl speaks to us across the centuries, warning us to respect our deep and fragile communal relationships within and among nations, and our meaningful relationships to the earth.

The past is not dead; it lives in our hearts, as myth lives in our hearts. We need those most human qualities of the world myths to help guide us on our road today.

My novel *Alburquerque* addresses some of these questions. The city where I live, like any other city in the Southwest, reflects the political processes that have permeated our land. The novel is about change, the change that has come during our lifetime. In it, some of the principal characters are driven by the desire to conquer the landscape, to control the land and the water of the Rio Grande. Others, members of the old tribes, take refuge in withdrawal in order to survive urban poverty. They withdraw to their circles of belief to wait out the storm.

We, the writers, cannot wait out the storm; we have to confront it. For us, the bedrock of beliefs of the old cultures provides our connection, our relationship. From that stance we must keep informing the public about the change that has come upon our land.

The battle is of epic proportions. We are in the midst of one of those times from which will emerge a new consciousness. The environment seems to reflect this struggle between evil and good; it cries out to us. We see it scarred and polluted. The people of the old tribes cry out; we see them displaced and suffering. Even the elements of nature reflect the change: acid and toxic chemicals pollute the water, nuclear waste is buried in the bowels of the earth. These are the same signs the Toltecs saw hundreds of years ago as their society faced destruction.

We, too, face a measure of destruction. The goal of material acquisition and a homogeneous political process supporting that goal have taken hold, driving us deeper into the complex nature of materialism. Is it any wonder we look back to legend and myth for direction?

We are poised at the edge of a new time. We have the opportunity to look again into the nature of our hemisphere. We can see that the struggle for illumination is not easy. It was not easy for the Toltecs, and we know now that as they gave up their old knowledge and turned to militarism and material gain, they destroyed their society.

Will we preserve our old values or let them die? Will we rediscover our relationship to the earth? What of the communal relationships that are so fractured and split in our land? Is there time to bring peace and harmony to our tribal groups?

The first step in answering these questions is to realize that we have turned away from our inner nature and from our connection to the earth and old historical relationships. We have allowed a political and economic consciousness from without to take control. How we engage this consciousness not only describes us but also will inform future generations of our values. Our writings will say where we stood when this drama of opposing forces came to be played out on our land.

LEO MARX

Open Spaces, City Places, and Contrasting Versions of the American Myth

I assume that the question we are addressing is not whether writers should attend to open spaces—what is often called "nature"—rather than to cities; not whether the countryside is more important than the city. Those strike me as wrongheaded ways to put the issue. The fact is that both city and countryside are important, and both have enemies—in many cases the same enemies. In any event, my first obligation as a cultural historian is to establish the fact that this way of thinking—posing an ostensible choice between open spaces and city places—has, like all other aspects of human experience, its own significant history. Part of that history is distinctively American, and though we can ignore it, pretend that it doesn't exist, we cannot avoid its implications.

That history is unavoidable because, for one thing, it is inscribed in our language, and therefore in our systems of meaning, value, and belief. As a result of our late-twentieth-century awareness of discourse as a social construction allied to related sets of practices—hence a recognition that our language bears the imprint of the cultural and historical circumstances in which it took form—we cannot assume that the words we are about to use—words like *city, countryside, open space, nature, desert*—merely provide direct, unambiguous, neutral referents to the ostensible entities we are discussing. Words do not constitute a transparent vehicle of communication. As Mikhail Bakhtin, one of the more influential modern literary theorists, put it: "Any discourse finds the object at which it was directed already overlain with qualifications open to dispute, charged with value, enveloped in an obscuring mist."

Let me try to dispel a little of that obscuring mist by placing the issue—"Open Spaces or City Places?"—in its historical context. I want to suggest that our ideas about the relations between cities and open spaces derive in part from the dominant European-American myth of national origins—American origins. I use the word "myth" here not in the currently popular sense of false belief but, rather, as a large ordering system of ideas, values, and meanings implicit in an archetypal narrative.

Our American myth of origins (it has several variants) turns on a familiar event: the migration of white Europeans from Europe to North America. Like any other myths, those formed around this narrative embody a plausible relation to a generally received account of historical reality. If they did not, they couldn't possibly gain a hold on the collective imagination. Many Europeans did in fact change their lives by electing to cross the Atlantic; we all take that for granted. Like all myths, however, the various myths of American origins distort that historical reality. Thus the notion that Europeans—or that Christopher Columbus—"discovered" the New World distorts the narrative by lending it, among other things, a quasi-racist cast. It implies that the European migrants came to a vacant North America, and accordingly that no account need be taken of the continent's existing inhabitants. There is no place, no positive role, in this myth for Native Americans who already were on the scene, and who were perceived as a part of the untamed wilderness, or for Afro-Americans, whose migration, far from a freely chosen act of liberation, was coerced.

In the moral geography nurtured by this myth, the migrating Europeans move westward, away from a built environment (which may be represented by, say, a grid or a city) toward a natural environment (which may be represented by a wild, open, unimproved, natural landscape). In this mythic geography the original meanings of cities and of open spaces are traceable to the aboriginal contrast between the Old World and the New World. Thus Europe is associated with London, Paris, and Rome—with history and an ancient urban civilization—whereas the "deserts" of North America (as the New World often was called) were identified with raw nature, with the nonhuman, which included "savages," open space, and prehistory. I want to identify three variants of this basic myth of national origins.

First, the dominant version may be called the *progressive* myth of America, although the explicit idea of "progress" didn't actually figure in this discourse until the late eighteenth or early nineteenth century. Here the positive values of civilization are set in opposition to the negative values of nature, and the result is a simple view of history as a record of continuous, cumulative, steady improvement in the human condition. Thus the transit of Europeans to the New World represents an expansion of the area in which the arts (both fine and practical) are practiced—the area, in other words, of increasing social complexity, refinement, civility, order, and sophistication. To settle the New World was to subjugate unruly, menacing nature, the realm of ignorance, illiteracy, disorder, and naïveté.

By the nineteenth century this version of the myth had flowered into the full-blown belief in progress. Its American slogans included "the conquest of nature," the "march of progress," and "Manifest Destiny." The final crystallization of the modern idea of progress by men like Condorcet and Turgot coincided with the three great revolutions of the late eighteenth century: the American, the French, and the industrial. Its germ is the idea of a steady, cumulative expansion of human knowledge of, and power over, nature. This sense of history, reinforced by association with a popularized Darwinian idea of human evolution as biological progress, provided a rationale for a program of the most rapid acceleration possible in the rate of science-based technological innovation. This viewpoint was immensely appealing to all the beneficiaries—especially those who shared in the new industrial wealth—of scientific and technological innovation.

It should be said, however, that the idea of progress changed over time. For the generation of the founding fathers—for men like Franklin, Jefferson, and Paine—the advances in science and technology were affirmed as being in the service of republican values. These men were revolutionary republicans, and to them progress meant liberation from the ancien régime—from monarchic, aristocratic, and ecclesiastical tyranny. At the outset, in other words, the advance of science and technology was endorsed as a means to a political and social end: the creation of a more just, humane, and peaceful society. If we could trace the changes in the dominant idea of progress from the early republic to the Reagan era, I believe we would see the atrophy of the old conception of scientific and technological progress as a means to a political end, and its replacement by a commitment to such progress as an end in itself—what might be called a technocratic (as opposed to a moral, political, or societal) idea of progress. Along the way we have followed men like Frederick Winslow Taylor, father of scientific management, who applied the methods of scientific analysis to all forms of human endeavor, especially work, with the result that we now are encouraged to adopt an uncritical respect for growth, development, and productivity as primary social goals.

Second, another version of the American myth was more appealing to those who were less privileged and, in many cases, expressly discontented. Here the locus of meaning and value was shifted from civilization to nature, so that the transatlantic migration was seen both as an escape from the negative significance of the Old World (oppression, scarcity, hierarchy, war, or, in a word, history) and as a quest for a more satisfying alternative. Hence the open space of the New World was invested with ideal significance: freedom, justice, peace, tolerance. In its extreme form, when these values are located in unmodified nature, this version of the myth of America is an expression of *primitivism*. On this view, the highest values are located as far as possible, in space or time or both, from the great urban centers of European civilization. Such an extremist doctrine, apart from a few hermetic types and literary characters, had very few adherents—at least among the white European colonizers. The only true primitivists among us—and even they qualified as such only in the eyes of European-Americans—were called "Indians."

Third, the impulse to escape from the constraints of the Old World produced, instead of primitivism, a mediating version of the myth closely associated with the tradition of the literary pastoral. The locus of meaning and value here is an ideal combination of the best of nature with the best of art: neither the wilderness nor the city but a landscape of reconciliation—a harmoniously modified "natural" landscape. For Thomas Jefferson, like many other Americans, the ideal state resembled colonial Virginia (for white people only, to be sure), with its ideal mixture of nature and art. Good books and French wines and no arrogant monarchs, aristocrats, or priests.

Here the appeal of open spaces, or the natural, has as much to do with what is not there (crowding, poverty, class tensions, militarism, social complexity) as with its actual and potential attributes. But the pastoral landscape also served as a repository of values that had been attributed to the presence of divinity: beauty, order, harmony, serenity, transcendence. According to the pastoral (as opposed to the primitivist) version of the myth, the movement away from European civilization is, up to a point, a movement toward freedom. But only up to a point. If pursued too zealously, this centrifugal motion almost certainly will lead to an encounter with omnipotent natural forces and, ultimately, with death.

This version of the myth forms the structural basis for some of the outstanding works of classic American literature, the sequence of pastoral romances that leads from *Walden* and *Huckleberry Finn* to *The Sun Also Rises* and *The Great Gatsby*. Each features a hero who initially finds himself in a state of alienation from a complex society and moves out, both as an escape and as a quest for an alternative way of life, in the direction of spaces identified with nature. The central part of the action consists of an exploration of those spaces as the potential, or imagined, locus of an alternative way of life. In the end, after a series of episodes, some of them more or less conventional, the protagonist manages an ambiguous or equivocal return. Many of our great pastoral romances are pastorals of failure. The disengagement, at first so hopeful, fails to yield sufficient fruits. But pastoralism, compared with primitivism or revolutionary political ideologies, is a relatively benign expression of discontent with the reigning culture.

Here we come to the vexed issue of American exceptionalism. We live in the only advanced industrial society that has never developed a militant anti-capitalist movement of the working class, or an effective political party dedicated to supplanting capitalism with socialism or communism, or an influential segment of the intelligentsia committed to Marxism. In part this is due to the apparent success of democratic capitalism in satisfying the material needs of a large fraction of the population. Whatever the reason, the political consciousness of Americans has taken a distinctive form in our time; this has something to do, I believe, with the special meanings attached to various images of the landscape as tokens of value.

In any case, we cannot talk about the relative significance of city places and open spaces as if these concepts referred, directly and unambiguously, to contrasting settings or topographies—as if they were not charged with historical significance. In fact they are deeply embedded in preestablished views or ideologies—each related to a version of the

myth of American origins. I have mentioned the progressive, the primitivist, and the pastoral versions, and there are others. But the point I
want to stress is that we are not discussing the choice of literary "settings" in any strict, narrow sense of the word. For a writer can lend approval or disapproval to any version of the myth in works that invoke
any of those settings—urban, rural, or wild. The choice of setting for
works of imaginative literature strikes me as a relatively unimportant,
or at least a secondary, issue compared with the writer's attitude toward
his or her valuation of that symbolic setting. A novel or poem set in the
city may convey either a positive or a negative view of the city, the view
belonging, as it were, to a literary tradition informed by either the progressive or the pastoral versions of the myth of national origins. The
crucial issue is not what setting the writer chooses but what sense of life
he or she embodies in the work, his or her notions about what does or
does not matter—and especially what matters most.

It is worth noting that we have had no American writers of
distinction—at least I cannot think of any—who have given unqualified
approval to the dominant myth of progress, with its tacit endorsement
of limitless growth and technological advance. I found Steward Udall's
eloquent tribute to our nation's institution of public lands—land owned
by the government—as a unique bulwark against greed, rapacity, and
mindless development extremely enlightening. Although he never used
the word "capitalism" or "socialism," it is interesting to consider the
political implications of his argument. He said that the only force capable of protecting the unspoiled countryside from degradation is the
government—which ostensibly is the only institution capable of repre-
senting the interests of the people as a collectivity. What also strikes me
is that the same deleterious forces of unbridled capitalism, from which
only the government can protect us, are in Udall's view as threatening
to our cities as they are to the countryside.

It might be useful to those who worry about what is happening to
the beautiful Arizona countryside to think about what is happening to
the central cities of New York, Detroit, and Boston. Our central cities
suffer from the effects of forces not unlike those represented by the un-
scrupulous developers who alarm so many lovers of the Southwest's
open spaces. Nor is the problem peculiar to Arizona or the United
States. It is quite possible to imagine similar discussions being held under the auspices of the Green Party in Germany, or similar groups in

Mexico or Brazil. All of which is to say, again, that the problem concerning us is not, at bottom, the problem of choosing among urban, rural, and wild settings but, rather, of controlling the powerful economic organizations, institutions, or forces that Udall sees as a kind of juggernaut. Come to think of it, it's a global juggernaut, and it threatens much more than the lovely landscape of Arizona.

OPEN SPACES

Mooney Falls, Havasu Canyon, Arizona. (Photograph © Stephen Trimble)

FREDERICK TURNER

Henry Thoreau Eats a Lizard: Writing the Land, Living the City

However much he may seem to them a shadowy, fugitive sort, the writer shares with his fellow mortals the inescapable condition of living always in two worlds. There is the somatic world, the world encased by skin, and there is the external world that supplies sustenance and stimuli. What distinguishes the writer from the nonwriter in this regard is a matter of degree, not kind, for the writer not only inhabits these two worlds but also must make an active virtue of this shared necessity, creatively exploiting the tension between the inner and the outer. For many writers this occupational hazard proves at last unbearable. Thus the parables of suicides from Thomas Chatterton to Sylvia Plath. Thus also the sad stories of those who were alcoholics, drug addicts, womanizers, compulsive risk takers, and so on. Then there are these apparently innocuous anecdotes of the habits of writers. This one wrote standing up, that one in bed. This one composed with a rotten apple in his desk, that one could work only in noisy public places. One began the day sharpening forty pencils, another's day could begin only after everybody else had gone to bed for the night. What are these anecdotes, really, but manifestations of the tension between the inner and outer worlds and the writer's pathetic—or is it heroic?—efforts at some sort of adjustment?

Writing asks a lot, and it is for this primitive reason that the writer is always searching for the set of living conditions that gives the greatest promise of easing the problems of his or her calling. Whatever conditions tend to soothe the tension of inhabiting two worlds so intensely, the writer will take pains to acquire them, even if this should involve deceit, crime, or the destruction of others' lives. To be sure, there are writers who find difficult, even dangerous, conditions advantageous. B. Traven, it is said, did his best work in the depths of a Chiapas jungle with all sorts of insects and reptiles whizzing and slithering about his workbench. And there can be no doubt that a certain hardness— whether of room or schedule or even chair—is a necessary defense against an easeful and unproductive sloth. But for all the monkishness some impose on themselves, writers are looking for conditions that may minimize their chronic unease rather than promote it. For instance, field notes made in the desert will be more readily shaped toward final form in a study than on the beautiful and unforgiving ground of their origin. One of the inherent peculiarities of what is now called "nature writing" is that it is almost never completed in situ but, rather, in some remove of civilization, because writing is tough enough without having to contend at the same time with demands of the unimproved external world.

These are essentially existential problems that writers face, and by themselves they surely would be quite enough to handle. But there may also be problems writers face by virtue of nationality; and in what is now the United States these have been unique, both because of the circumstances of settlement and because of the nature of that exterior world to which the settlers came.

Those settlers were essentially products of an urban-centered civilization. By the seventeenth century, Europe and the British Isles still contained considerable amounts of "unimproved" land as well as a good deal of acreage in agricultural production. But the great forests that had once covered the Old World had been pruned back, the marshes drained and filled. The landscape had been conquered and tamed, and the locus of human thought and energy had shifted to the urban centers. Already the percentage of those who made their living directly from the land was smaller than that of those who were middlemen, dealers, tradespeople, or industrial workers. Moreover, even for those still on the land, the system of trade using money had in most places supplanted the ancient system of barter using commodities; and both the newer system and its currency derived from the city to which the commodities now flowed.

The city had also become the intellectual center of the Old World, the seat of learning. Here were the first significant libraries, repositories of accumulated and shared learning. The city was the center for art, the place to which aspiring artists, writers, and musicians went in their efforts to establish themselves. Finally, the city was the place in which the technology was assembled and applied that made possible the grand enterprise of exploration and settlement. Thus, regardless of individual backgrounds, the settlers who came to the New World were products of a city-centered civilization, and their first concerted activity as settlers was to huddle together and build towns (those potential cities) to supply the sudden lack of those things they may not even have guessed they owed the city. And when some of them pushed out from the towns to the frontier, they often did so of necessity, not by choice: as Crèvecoeur showed in his deft analysis of the settled and the mobile in eighteenth-century America, it was the have-nots and riffraff who moved on ahead of civilization.

What was true for the settlers in general was true in spades for the writers and artists who came here. They came carrying the traditions, habits, and preferences of the city. They were comfortable with the city and in it, however much the natural world might figure in their work. The ancient substratum of land- and sea-based mythology that is the bedrock of Old World literature had long since become city property, providing writers and artists with a deep fund of metaphors and plots. But it had been a long time, really, since the *primary* inspiration in the arts had come from encounters with the unimproved natural world. Socrates is alleged to have said that fields and trees "teach me nothing, but the people of a city do"; and many American writers of the seventeenth and eighteenth centuries would have agreed, feeling suddenly, not the potential imaginative fruitfulness of nature but the absence of evident signs of "culture," their stock-in-trade. Suddenly, as it must have seemed to them, they found themselves forced to create in a shaggy, unshorn sort of vacuum, without ateliers, libraries, coffeehouses; perhaps worst was the absence of those loose but significant associations of kindred spirits talking art and literature, sparking each other in debate. There was only the great land, waiting, apparently voiceless, historyless, and, if not actively hostile, then a heavy, inert mass with which the writer had to struggle.

These well-rehearsed facts serve to explain why genuine literary assents to the landscape were slow to develop in what was to become known as "Nature's Nation"; they also serve to remind us why in

America the only literatures primarily inspired by the natural world have been tribal ones. For the rest—Hispanic, Anglo, Afro-American—it was the city the writers longed for, would live in, would flee the land for as soon as they could. American nature was for a long time at best a backdrop—as it was also in American painting until the time of Thomas Cole. I believe it was D. H. Lawrence—that brilliant guesser—who first drew attention to this inevitable phenomenon and suggested that it was responsible for that edginess, that chronic tension evident in the works of our "classic" authors: as if they had had to write with the great land looking over their shoulders like a judging specter, waiting to see if what they scrawled could possibly be equal to their existential opportunity in these virginal climes.

We might do worse than consider Henry David Thoreau as an individual example of this shared condition. Our literature of landscape—of a deep, imaginative engagement with American nature—may be said to have begun with him. Certainly I find nothing like his work in the previous century of American writing (William Bartram comes closest). Still, when we assess Thoreau's career, it is difficult to imagine how he might ever have worked out his relationship to the land—to say nothing of a viable literary esthetic—without the mediating aids of his Harvard education and his ready access to libraries. To be sure, the terms of his learning were very much his own, yet it was learning that can ultimately be traced back to the city that he creatively applied to his encounters with the woods and waters of New England. Moreover, Thoreau, like other writers of his time and subsequently, had to look to the city for the production of his work as well as for potential consumers of it. He would address, he said, all America, yet he knew from his travels in New England that those who lived closest to nature were, oddly, the ones least disposed to appreciate what he was writing.

For all his yearning toward the wild, his genuine desire to give a true report of the west side of the mountain, Thoreau at last found himself a writer with unbreakable bonds to the city and its gifts. He would turn his back on the city and walk westward, but he knew the city was behind him, backing him, that it was his to return to. Out at Walden Pond he tells us that he once came across a woodchuck

> and felt a strange thrill of savage delight, and was strongly tempted to seize
> and devour him raw. . . . I found, and still find, an instinct toward a higher,

or, as it is named, spiritual life, as most men do, and another toward a primitive rank and savage one, and I reverence them both. I love the wild not less than the good.[1]

The language here, with its fond old oppositions—higher versus savage, good versus wild—suggests what was the truth about Thoreau and his yearning for the wild: that it was the yearning of a man whose primary reference was the city, civilization. Here is a hard primitivism—of which he had read. It has, as Thoreau learned up in Maine, somewhat less to do with the realities of aboriginal life in the woods than he had supposed, and when he made contact with those realities, they were not altogether pleasing. At the end of the "Chesuncook" chapter of what posthumously became *The Maine Woods*, he freely confesses that it was a "relief to get back to our smooth, but still varied landscape. For a permanent residence, it seemed to me that there could be no comparison between this and the wilderness, necessary as the latter is for a resource and a background, the raw material of all our civilization."[2]

Can there be anywhere a more seminal and poignant presentation of the unique circumstances of the American writer than this one by a man who struggled throughout his career to apprehend the vast cultural contradiction he sensed lurking in such an attitude? Here in "Nature's Nation" the unimproved natural world could truly serve the writer only as metaphor and as an occasionally visited place of renewal, not as a real residence and diet. One does not actually eat the woodchuck, raw or cooked, except in one's imagination. One retreats gratefully from the grim and shaggy wilderness to the smooth comforts of civilization, there to write about the tonic of the wild.

Thoreau was no sophist, nor do I attempt by these words to make him seem so. He was an honest man who kept trying on his successive excursions—to the Maine woods again, to the West in 1861—to come to a fuller accommodation with the wild. He was in this sense perhaps the truest American writer white civilization has yet produced. The knot he found in his Maine woods manuscript was that uneasy and superficial-seeming relationship between the writer in the New World and the New World itself. He was still trying to untie it in his last months as he worked valiantly on the revisions, muttering with his last breath, "Moose . . . Indian . . . ."

With an equal brevity let me turn to the example of John Muir, of whom it is often said, as it is of Thoreau, that no writer owed less to the city or was more fundamentally antagonistic to it. Intimately connected with the natural world as he became on his long, solitary, often hazardous excursions into it, Muir would never have become the writer he did without the influence of the city. Nor would he have become a published writer had he made good on his oft-stated determination to remain up in the mountains, away from San Francisco.

In the penal servitude of his years on his father's Wisconsin farm, it was the long arm of the city that reached out to him amid the corn rows when he first read European Romantic literature. In the records of that explosive encounter between the modern city and the subdued landscape, Muir found clues to the meaning of his own existence. Reading how flowers and fields had soothed the city-chafed men of the Old World, Muir looked anew on the landscape of his own drudgery; nature was never the same for him thereafter. Later, at the University of Wisconsin, it was the scientific researches of European city men that intrigued him. Still later, he came to Emerson and Thoreau. Up in the Sierra it was these influences that provided the specific terms of his insights into glaciers and water ouzels, though like Thoreau his applications were distinctive. Acknowledging the Romantics and the great figures of nineteenth-century science as major influences, Muir never acknowledged the urban context of that influence; but it is there nevertheless. However much Muir may appear to be in the line of Zen philosophy or American Indian thought, Romantic literature and nineteenth-century science—Agassiz, Lyell, Humboldt, Darwin—provided him with compass bearings he never lost.

The point is not so much the continuity of influences—though with Muir this is interesting. The point is, rather, that even one of our most renegade writers, who traveled farthest out and seemed to shun both the city and all of white civilization, appears on a closer inspection to have been profoundly indebted to both. Muir had objected vehemently to Ruskin and his writing on mountains because he thought Ruskin a mere sojourner in the Alps, a man distinctly of the city who went out for a look at mountains and then retreated to the comforts of the city to write about them. "He is fettered and bound," Muir wrote of Ruskin from Yosemite Valley, "though his chain is long."[3] Yet three years after writing this, Muir discovered that he, too, had a chain tied to him and that it led back to San Francisco. For he had by now discovered that he was a writer, and that a writer has different needs, different obligations than a mountaineer does. The books he had so loved, that he had packed with him into the highest, most inaccessible reaches of the Sierra proved to have for him unsuspected entailments. Products of the city, they ultimately led back to it.

Distasteful as it was for him initially to contemplate the new prospect, Muir saw more and more that his career was to write in the city for those who had not had his wilderness advantages. Besides, as he moved steadily toward middle age, he saw the truth the aged Emerson had pointed out to him in Yosemite years earlier: that wilderness solitude made a beguiling mistress but an intolerable wife. "Bless me," he wrote on the verge of his descent into San Francisco, "what an awful thing town duty is! I was once free as any pine-playing wind, and I feel that I have still a good length of line, but alack! there seems to be a hook or two of civilization in me that I would fain pull out, *yet would not pull out*—O,O,O!!!"[4]

Can we imagine a literature owing *nothing* to the city and its culture, whose inspiration derives from the land itself, whose reference, so to say, goes back to the land that inspired the work? Reading translations of aboriginal literatures will be as close as many of us can ever get to such an experience. In the celebrated Seneca myth often translated as "The Story-Telling Stone," the land is described as speaking to the people and telling them of their history. Here the circuit of reference arcs from the land to the people and back again to the land. There is no other temporal sphere imagined or, indeed, extant in which either teller or audience has a camp, to which retreat may be made in order to comment on the world of forest and stone. True, here, as in other tribal myths, there is the spirit world, but it is always seen as part of a unified tribal cosmos. Changes of form, movement upward through three dim underworlds to emerge into the world of sun and mesas—all this happens within a traditionally unified cultural context, and there is never imagined some other earthly place where the conditions of tribal life might be escaped or abrogated. *This*, the myths tell us, is the way things are and must be. These are literatures of one world.

In the very unity of these tribal worlds, reflected in the ancient narratives, we see also the vulnerability of these worlds, how easily they might be penetrated by those who for some time had been able to exist in an urban-centered civilization while restlessly pushing out into the unhallowed and voiceless spaces of a New World they would soon re-make into a facsimile of the Old. In the moment when Spanish anchors hissed into the Antilles' opalescent depths, the unity of these tribal worlds was doomed, and in the long aftermath American Indians have had to learn how to create narratives all over again, this time narratives of two worlds: the remembered earth and its traditions, and the world the whites made, with its cities and their multiple extensions. It seems Momaday, Silko, Vizenor, Tapahonso, Ortiz, and other contemporary Indian writers are in the process of showing us all how we can write about the American earth in a way that recaptures something of its old magic, that very magic so misunderstood and so fiercely resisted by the first settlers and their writers. While we are listening to them to catch the cadences, the themes, and the vision that can comprehend both Sun City and the Sonoran Desert, I like to think back on Henry Thoreau and his own vision quest that was interrupted by death.

One day while walking in the hills above Santa Fe, I quickly sketched in my mind Thoreau's *Southwestern Journals*. I saw him in Minnesota in 1861, still searching for some way to harmonize his writer's world—or possibly some new landscape that would harmonize it for him. Then I saw him turn, not eastward, with the damp seal of a tubercular death stamped on his brow, but west, whither, he said in "Walking," his steps always unconsciously tended. I saw him going down the Mississippi by boat to St. Louis and then overland through Kansas to New Mexico and Santa Fe. But in Santa Fe for the winter he finds he is bored with beds, with any kind of quarters, as if he were awakening from a long and troubled sleep. His riddled lungs are already beginning to heal and expand; he feels he needs air, and thus leaves the huddled town. Still west into Arizona and the Sonoran desert as spring comes on with a burning dryness his whole being welcomes: the sky! the blue moun-tains! He is too wise to disparage his old New England landscape in the presence of this spectacular new one, but still he feels here a true and undivided assent to where he is. One morning he catches a lizard—chuckwalla, fringe-toed—up from its burrow to take the sun. But by this time he knows he doesn't have to devour it raw in order to get the full flavor.

NOTES

1. Henry David Thoreau, "Higher Laws," in *Walden*, in *The Portable Thoreau*, Carl Bode, ed. (New York: Penguin Books, 1947, 1981), 457.

2. Henry David Thoreau, *The Maine Woods* (New York: Thomas Y. Crowell, 1961), 203.

3. John Muir, letter to J. B. McChesney, January 9, 1873 (Yosemite National Park Research Library).

4. John Muir, letter to Jeanne C. Carr, July 1875, John Muir Papers (Holt-Atherton Library, University of the Pacific).

PETER WILD

Pornography and Nature

Recently one of my colleagues, a quite sophisticated lady, yowled at a revelation about John C. Van Dyke, though it was entirely by accident that I caused her such pain.

Van Dyke, as she knew, and as some of you also might know, is the author of *The Desert*. Published in 1901, it was a path-breaking book, the first to celebrate, instead of denigrate, America's arid sweeps. Until then, the public all but uniformly despised such vast places as the Devil's domain. They were the haunts of travelers' bones, as many fearsome pioneer accounts bear witness. In fact, useless as they were for human gain except for occasional gold strikes and such, the dry and cracking wastelands made the otherwise faithful scratch their heads over God's intentions in creating them. Had the hand of Providence slipped? Maybe so, was the occasional heretical observation. For instance, this apostrophe of Gothic doubt over the Deity's emotional state:

> Some lengthwise sun-dried shapes with feet and hands
> And thirsty mouths pressed on the sweltering sands,
> Mark here and there a gruesome graveless spot
> Where some one drank thy scorching hotness, and is not.
> God must have made these in His anger, and forgot.[1]

Desert newcomer John C. Van Dyke opposed this melancholy view with cultural radicalism. Instead of scowling, he celebrates the desert as a wonderland. To him, it is an endless and ineffable canvas, painted by a quite rational Almighty at His most inspired moment. For, summarizes Van Dyke, with a desert "you have the most decorative landscape in the world, a landscape all color, a dream landscape."[2] So instead of cursing, the writer rhapsodizes over the lands of little rain, penning, as some students have said of *The Desert*, a book-length prose poem in praise. Thus Lawrence Clark Powell affirms, and almost all other scholars of Southwestern literature echo, that Van Dyke "said it first and said it best."[3] Van Dyke's volume occupies a central place in desert literature, for it is the mentor of all those other books by desert-loving writers so familiar to us, from Mary Austin down through Joseph Wood Krutch, and on to Edward Abbey.

So much my friend knew, but hearing over lunch one day that I was doing research on the author of *The Desert*, she paused with a spoonful of cheese soup trailing its strands in midair to ask about the writer of the Southwest's famous book. Who was John C. Van Dyke? How had he come to the desert?

Whether this was graciousness or genuine curiosity on her part, I don't know. But as usual in such situations, she got more than she bargained for. She had made the mistake of showing interest in a scholar's project.

In the next few minutes, I raced through Van Dyke's career with hardly a gasp for breath. I touched on his refined background, on his long family line of righteous and prosperous Dutch ancestors dating back to the New Amsterdam of the seventeenth century. Elaborating on this, I pointed proudly to his education at Columbia, his position as a professor of art history at Rutgers College, and his concurrent tenure as head librarian at the nearby New Brunswick Theological Seminary. To spice up the rundown, I dipped into Van Dyke's youthful and still mysterious frolickings as a cowboy in Wyoming and Montana. I leapt ahead to paint a vignette of the gentlemanly art critic having a civilized day of trout fishing with Andrew Carnegie and other wealthy poohbahs near the industrialist's castle in Scotland. Further to impress her while completing the sketch, I ticked off the titles of some of Van Dyke's more than forty books, fine books highly successful in his day but now, regrettably, all but forgotten in the shadow of *The Desert*.

I paused. She seemed interested, so I went on, delving into the finer points of the critic's aesthetic views. A devotee of art for art's sake, Van

Dyke held that beauty is the highest good and that, furthermore, nature is its highest revelation. Thus, it was only natural that this connoisseur would write *The Desert* the way he did. Traveling west in the late 1890s from New Jersey, in hopes of finding relief from his asthma in the dry desert air, the middle-aged professor did what he always did when he traveled, whether in the United States, Europe, Russia, Asia Minor, or the Orient. The popular writer who turned out one volume, sometimes two, a year for Scribner's wrote a book about what he saw. And what he saw, in the desert as elsewhere, was what he was prepared to see: that nature represents the highest art.

"So you see," I said, opening my arms expansively at the end of my mini lecture, "Van Dyke simply applied his art for art's sake values, learned in the drawing rooms of the refined East, to these hellish masses of cacti and burning ash heaps that surround us."

But as so often happens with the fruits of my researches, what I'd intended as an intellectual blessing flew like an arrow into my friend's heart. "Stop! Stop!" she cried. "You mean Van Dyke didn't come out here as a refugee from civilization, to be converted by the desert's lonesome beauty?" I cringed before her continued attack: "That instead this Lord Fauntleroy of the art world, all the while wearing a lily in his breast pocket, came out here with his mind made up and imposed his effete Eastern values on what he saw, and that's how we got *The Desert?*"

"Well," I demurred, trying to calm her and at the same time maintain historical accuracy, "that part about the lily isn't exactly right, and . . . ." Then I admitted, eyes downcast and seeing it was useless, "Well, yes, that's about the gist of it." The damage was irreparable. Unwittingly, I'd insulted one of her heroes.

But not really insulted her hero so much as insulted her *image* of him. And from that I think you catch the drift of where this discussion on pornography and nature might be headed. I race to say that my central observation is not original. Other students of the culture have stated it nobly. Nor is its essence especially complex. But I do think the idea may have profound consequences in its application. So I'd like to turn it around and see it from slightly different angles than others have viewed it, particularly as regards desert writer John C. Van Dyke. A mean spirit does not lurk behind my motive; I'm not dedicated to pricking emotional balloons floating over the desert specifically or over nature in general. However, consideration of the idea may help enrich our appreciation of the home that sustains us—all of us physically, and a good many of us spiritually.

It comes down to this: though the world's a complex place, our minds tend to view it simply. That is, bombarded by the tangles of often conflicting information that make up our daily experiences, we're overwhelmed. As a result, we do the human thing. We latch onto one of the aspects floating past and accept that small part as the whole. It should be said that there is survival value in this. If we tried to understand all the complexities around us, we'd be stymied—stuck for days, weeks, maybe a whole lifetime, trying to figure out the meaning of what may be relatively inconsequential to our affairs. After all, when we nod to a fellow worker in the morning and say, "How're you doing today?" we neither expect nor desire a truthful reply. We'd be taken aback if our co-worker seized us and launched into a heartfelt lament over the state of his or her marriage or his or her worry over the root canal scheduled for next Thursday. Though we like to think of ourselves as caring and sensitive people, we don't have time for that; there's work to do. We expect, usually get, and give in return, "Fine. How are you?" or something equally bland. We simplify out of necessity.

Then, too, it's probably just as well that we don't always strive to look far down the road into the mists of complexities before us. Considering all the possible ramifications of falling in love, buying a house, or changing jobs might be so frightening as to leave us inert and dumbfounded. Instead, we simplify and plunge ahead, trusting to the angels to save us.

Yet life being the precarious thing that it is, there's a double, if not a triple, disadvantage to all this simplifying, to not being in the least aware of the complexities behind our actions and concepts. As individuals, and collectively as a society, we pay for the convenience. We can't be experts at everything, yet when we trip gaily down the path of oversimplification, sometimes we hornswoggle ourselves. "Let's buy it," coos our wife, clutching our arm, buoyed by the charm of a charming old adobe house with arched windows and an orange tree in the patio. In the face of her enthusiasm, we don't want to be our standard, ogre selves. Besides, she's right. It *is* a charming place. We see ourselves picking fruit off the tree for our breakfast. With no mind for termites or rusted plumbing, we haul out the checkbook and buy the place. Then for years after, as we probe the crawl space—the webby kingdom of

black widows—with a flashlight, wincing at leaks and sagging founda-
tions, we curse our foolishness.

Worse still is when others hornswoggle *us*. Politicians, generals, and
admen take advantage of our weakness to get us to do what they want:
mostly to remain docile while they make the decisions. That nineteenth-
century worrier about the course of democracy, Alexis de Tocqueville,
fretted about it constantly. If he appeared in our midst, no doubt he
would rend his garments and pour ashes over his head at our childish,
bumper-sticker mentality. Buy This, Believe That, Hug Your Children,
Go Sailing. And what do we do? Off we march. Once we abandon ourselves to the mind-set, the jig's up.

I suppose that every society has to do one jig or another, and some
good comes of it, though often for the wrong reasons. For example,
James Watt backfired on the Reagan administration. The testy secretary
of the interior woke up a slumbering environmental movement. During
his vocally earth-spiteful tenure, membership in the Sierra Club soared
by tens of thousands. But though we can't look into human hearts, it
seems clear from political analysis that people rallied not so much out
of love for the earth as out of spite against Watt—the irony being that a
smoother operator would have kept us slumbering.

The worst rub, however, comes when we bamboozle ourselves,
joyously pirouetting toward our own destruction—leveling the forests
as we populate a continent, throwing poisons into the water we drink,
slurping up nature's underground reservoirs until, in amazement, we
watch the ground cracking beneath our feet.

The problem with such things, as with so many others, is that we're
pornographers all. To our peril, we consider nature simply rather than
complexly, grasping at one aspect to the exclusion of others, just as
some people salivate over alluring Pamela Jean Stein, a *Playboy* "Play-
mate of the Month." No matter that the young lady says she wants to
learn to play the bass guitar and tells us that she's addicted to lasagna
and turkey dressing. We're not interested in *that*. And neither, for the
moment, should we be. Let's face it. Miss Stein has a beautiful body, as
does nature, and what she's getting paid to offer us through the marvels
of wood pulp and color photography certainly is not a discourse on her
musical aspirations and her culinary preferences.

How we airbrush both nature and women! Is there much difference
in treatment between the lurid pinups decorating seedy barroom walls

and the coffee-table books in your living room and mine, lavish with their photographs of redwoods and snowcapped peaks? By over-simplifying, by concentrating on one aspect of reality, both make us suck in our breaths, both take us to the vertiginous limits of our desires. In this sense, *Bambi* is just as pornographic as *Deep Throat*.

Much ink has been expended on exploring and condemning the traditional parallel between women and nature, in faulting our references to "virgin forests" and mystical "Mother Nature" as signs of society's chauvinism. Don't worry; I'm not going to bore you by expending more ink on the issue. I take, in fact, a somewhat different view. Rather than flagellating ourselves, we should rejoice not only that the comparison is, in one sense, entirely valid but, furthermore, that we can have it both ways. In fact, I maintain that the best of our nature writers have done so.

I mean that the most celebrated nature writers, from the eighteenth century's James Thompson down through Thoreau, John Muir, and, in our own century, Mary Austin, Aldo Leopold, Annie Dillard, and Ann Zwinger, have had a double vision of nature. They've seen it both simply and complexly, the passion that attracts us grounded in good sense, their appealing romanticism propelled by science and vice versa. And to good effect, for the multidimensional approach to nature also is what prevents their work from lapsing into cliché and keeps the public reading their books. Muir, for example, could get out his pocket magnifying glass and count the number of hairs on a square inch of a bighorn sheep's hide. That didn't prevent him, however, from reveling in sometimes sticky language about the exhilarations of scaling Sierra peaks. Leopold, trained as a scientist, brought his education at Yale to bear on nature, only to discover an endless succession of mysteries opening before him. That is precisely the appeal of such writers. From them we learn that nature indeed is mysterious, not only from the perspective of the romantic out for quick thrills on a stroll but also from that of an unending series of mysteries that surrounds us when we view the natural world through the rationalist's glass. By either route we come to romance, and both as readers and as Sunday escapees from the city to hiking trails we are richer for the double vision.

It's second nature for us humans to embody our awe in some object, some symbol. For writers, the impulse can mean death to their work if they drag out the old, worn icons—in our case, nature as woman. But it also can set their words quivering if they give an old object added dimensions that it ordinarily lacks. To see this latter aspect at work, let's return to our desert friend, John C. Van Dyke.

Throughout his books, Van Dyke refers to nature as "she," and I suppose some contemporary writers, at the first whiff of that spoor, might take off after him with malice in their hearts. To do so, however, would be hasty and anti-intellectual, would be to overlook the subtleties in his complex reconstruction of an old image, a romantic reconstruction firmly based on science.

Part of it Van Dyke imposed, part he learned. What he imposed, his given, comes from his devotion to art for art's sake. As we noted, this holds that the appreciation of beauty is life's highest goal—burn with a "hard gem-like flame," advocated Walter Pater, English mouthpiece for the movement. Van Dyke, along with other disciples, found his best fuel in nature. Scrambling up a rocky Western slope, Van Dyke discovers a "pale-pink flower on a long thin stem." Rhapsodizing at some length in *The Open Spaces* over "pale beauties that blush unseen," he lapses into the cliché of his day through the implied comparison of nature to passive women.[4] For what it is, the passage is heady and nobly stated, but it is not Van Dyke at his most original moment.

If the traveling art critic from Rutgers did no more than present us with the vision of nature as a sedate, Victorian damsel, I would not be talking about him here—and neither would people be reading him today. Nature as an attractive young lady dressed in pastels, however, is but one aspect of Van Dyke's feminine nature imagery. The young lady is not a simpleton. Under other conditions, she suddenly turns into a seductress, thus embodying two other qualities we seek in the wilds, wonder expanding into awe. The unexplored and the ever-changing lured Van Dyke into nature with "a mad fascination." Ever-shifting, unpredictable nature constantly thrilled him with her shifting guises. Lying in his sleeping bag, far from civilization, the bachelor traveler finds his lover. For as the stars rush overhead, he feels the wind stroking his body with a "loved woman's hands," thus wafting him into the oceanic feeling of being at last "at home in the infinite."[5]

So much the feisty critic might dismiss as the self-generated passions of the facile romantic. But remember: Van Dyke was no tourist seeking easy whimwhams in nature. His natural history—his comments on geology, botany, and zoology—is as accurate as the state of science of his day allowed it to be. When writing *The Desert*, for instance, he stopped in Tucson to check his desert knowledge with professors at the University of Arizona. Also, from long experience as a cowboy and from later excursions on horseback across the West, ranging from the Canadian border deep into Mexico, the trail-toughened art critic, for all his urban refinements, knew the land and its dangers firsthand. He set a cowboy's broken leg; traveling alone through the wilds of Arizona, he stood off a band of horse thieves; he defied nature's lottery by crossing the Colorado Desert, cheating death by digging in streambeds for life-saving water. From such experiences, Van Dyke knew that if nature is a mistress, she's a demanding one. She tolerates little weakness in her suitors. "In the wild," Van Dyke observes, "neither man nor beast pays any heed to the cry of the weak."[6]

With a Darwinian view of survival to counterbalance his equally strong romanticism, Van Dyke adds realistically that "the Great Mother," nature, "never hears, never heeds."[7] His seductive lover lures victims with her attractions, only to turn on them, "red in tooth and claw," as Tennyson reminds us—and as our scientific knowledge of the impersonal workings of the food chain confirms.

Yet even if one such as Van Dyke, by dint of luck and skill, survives, the great paramour is not done. Like a cat playing with its captured mouse, she toys with him, tempting him, trying to drive him mad with a vision of helplessness. She may be lovely, but in return for his atten-tions, she treats him with "contempt"[8] until, thus rebuffed, he wonders: "Are we anything more than petty animalculae clinging to a cold dis-carded fragment of a sun? You turn over in your blankets and listen to the yap of a distant coyote. Along that Milky Way lies madness."[9] Still, stumbling around in the desert, dazed by both hardship and beauty, the romantic lover tries to make contact:

> And quite as impressive as the mysteries are the silences. Was there ever such a stillness as that which rests upon the desert at night! Was there ever such a hush as that which steals from star to star across the firmament! You perhaps think to break the spell by raising your voice in a cry; but you will not do so again. The sound goes but a little way and then seems to come back to your ear with a suggestion of insanity about it.[10]

Indeed, for Van Dyke nature is a no one-dimensional Miss Pamela Jean Stein. His winsome lass keeps transmorgrifying herself from a frag-ile damsel to a Great Mother to a demon lover—and then, when least expected, assumes yet again an innocent coyness. These changing qualities, cruel as they may seem, cruel as they sometimes can be in the affairs of men and women, were what kept the tough-minded professor coming back to nature with "a mad fascination." His lover, nature, never slaked his cravings but instead led him on and on through the years until, looking back on a life spent largely in the outdoors, he declared—as do some of us about tempestuous loves with creatures of flesh and blood—that whatever the long turmoil, "Nature has proved the most lasting love of all."[11]

NOTES

1. Madge Morris, "The Colorado Desert," in George Wharton James, ed., *The Influence of the Climate of California upon Its Literature* (Pasadena, Calif.: The Author, 1912), 10.

2. John C. Van Dyke, *The Desert* (New York: Charles Scribner's Sons, 1901), 56.

3. Lawrence Clark Powell, *Southwest Classics: The Creative Literature of the Arid Lands—Essays on the Books and Their Writers* (Tucson: University of Arizona Press, 1974), 327.

4. John C. Van Dyke, *The Open Spaces* (New York: Charles Scribner's Sons, 1922), 130–131.

5. Ibid., 20.

6. John C. Van Dyke, *The Mountain* (New York: Charles Scribner's Sons, 1916), 3.

7. John C. Van Dyke, *Nature for Its Own Sake* (New York: Charles Scribner's Sons, 1901), 292.

8. Van Dyke, *The Desert*, 7.

9. Van Dyke, *The Open Spaces*, 19.

10. Van Dyke, *The Desert*, 107.

11. John C. Van Dyke, *The Raritan* (New Brunswick, N.J.: Privately printed, 1916), 86.

ANN H. ZWINGER

Space and Place

The title of this conference, "Open Spaces, City Places," emphasizes the separation between the ungridded "out there" open spaces and the constricted city spaces, and implies that the quality of life in the city is rather on the meager side. As Stewart Udall said in his essay, anybody with the smarts escapes to the country whenever possible.

I'd like to address this assertion as a nature writer who depends upon both worlds to write, who deplores the sentimentalization of nature as well as the trashing of the city. I do not believe in throwing myself on the bosom of Mother Earth and watering the ground with tears in catharsis, nor do I believe in discarding city life because it has become banal, brutal, and crime-ridden. But nonetheless there *is* a difference between city life and country life, and that very dichotomy makes it possible for me to write as I do and, I hope, to entertain those who do not wish to go out and commune with saguaros and whiptails, and to entice them to take a closer look at the natural world about them, to learn about it, and to be on its side when the decisions are made.

The philosophy that cities are ugly and nature is beautiful is a fairly recent development in the United States. In the nineteenth century people praised the glories of the city and damned nature. Nature was threatening and dark, evil lurked in those foreboding forests full of trees. Nature was to be gotten rid of so you could plant crops and survive, and doing so was often doing battle. The great outdoors was where no one wanted to be if it could be helped—humanity had so recently come indoors. Those men who preferred the wilderness to the city (God forbid a woman should have felt so) were outlanders, oddballs, who couldn't fit into society.

The city was the place to be. There one relished hot meals and gaslights, enjoyed companionship and put one's feet on the brass rail, cherished the ministrations of a doctor, looked at the alien world through lace curtains, blessed indoor plumbing; there the danger of encountering rattlesnakes or grizzlies was negligible.

Our generation tends to the opposite. We romanticize nature as the cure-all for all our stressful ills, as the place where anybody who is anybody eventually ends up, purified and sanctified. I've been unable to find when the phrase "Mother Nature" appeared in common usage. That term carries a lot of baggage and sums up the way humanity responds to nature: nurturing, protective, mothering. It is a term that amuses and dismays, for it personifies nature. It assumes a kindliness about nature that is not there. It gives me the willies because just saying the phrase connotes all kinds of images, none of which strike me as a healthy way of looking at the world in which we live. Our disaffection with town says that anyone who lives there is beleaguered, beset, and a little crazy. I daresay that many of those who extol the virtues of nature in the raw do so within arm's reach of the TV.

Personally, I disagree with both extremes. I am a city mouse as well as a country mouse. I utilize the amenities of the city while I deplore the desperate situation of our inner cities, recognize the crime rate, and know that I would not survive in those confines any more than I could survive totally alone for the rest of my life in the wilderness. Nevertheless, I appreciate fresh asparagus at the market, browse the bookshops, take aerobics classes, read by electric lights, freeze ice cubes, throw clean wash into the dryer, pump gas for my car, cook by turning a switch, and draw water by turning a faucet. I spend countless hours taking advantage of what the city provides, sitting in the wrong height chair in front of the wrong height CRT, taking endless research notes at the Colorado College library. Indeed, without the almost unlimited research opportunities of the city, I could not write as I do.

But without nature in the raw, I could not write—period, full stop. For the kind of writing I do, setting is primary. The hours I spend out-of-doors, and I mean *really* out—away from light switches, reliable water, limitless clean socks, plumbing, and a blinking word processor—are a small percentage of my year. I scanned my travel schedule for the last three years, when I was doing fieldwork for a book on deserts, and figured that I spent between five hundred and six hundred hours "out." Since there are 8,760 hours in a year, that comes down to less than 15 percent of my allotted yearly hours.

I recognize that these five hundred to six hundred hours bear more heavily on my life and understanding than the other 85 percent of my time. This disproportionate importance of the natural world in my life didn't soak in until 1987, and was impressed upon me by three disparate experiences: I taught a course in natural history writing at Colorado College; read a scholarly book by Annette Kolodny that documents how women coming West reacted to the landscape in which they found themselves, and the difference in their reactions vis-à-vis men; and gave a reading at the Poetry Center at the University of Arizona.

Colorado College is on the block system, which means that you have three and a half weeks in which to teach a given course, and it is the only course your students take. It is difficult to teach writing under those circumstances, for there is never enough time for work to settle, to be put aside long enough to come back to see it with new eyes. But it did allow us to go up into the mountains for several days each week— after all, if you're going to write about nature, you'd better be out in it. I wanted to develop students' powers of observation, teach them the nuts and bolts of taking notes and keeping a journal, and introduce them to the skills and elegance of editing.

I expected to find in their journals, and did, an expression of the dichotomy between town and country, the plagues of overbusy campus life, and the peace of aspen trees and sun-warmed gravel slopes. That's the party line these days. But I noted a subtle shift, a greater sincerity in their writing, as their ease with a place they saw and wrote about frequently grew. Rather than an unfounded romanticism, a realistic at-homeness with the out-of-doors surfaced that pleased me very much.

Concurrently I was reading Annette Kolodny's book, *The Land Before Her*, and realized that in my life I had paralleled the development of pioneer women in their approach to nature. She makes a strong statement that men were out to conquer, tame, in some cases rape, the natural world—if not in actuality, then in spirit.

Early pioneer women reacted quite differently. A few fitted into the sodbusters' life, but most revealed fear, loneliness, dismay, displacement in their diaries. They reacted by trying to bring what they knew from home, and the easiest things to bring were plants. They tried to make gardens, both for survival and for familiarity. That some came to feel at home was the result of that tremendous capacity inherent in the female of the species for acclimatization.

Reading Kolodny's book, I felt as if, in my lifetime, I had recapitulated a universal feminine experience in my reaction to landscape and the developing sense of at-homeness that my writing documents over the years.

I have to reach back to a childhood when the natural world was an alien and threatening place. I early demonstrated literary ingenuity and vivid imagination worthy of a novelist in the voluminous letters I wrote to my mother so that she would remove me from the life of terror in camp, penning vivid descriptions of galloping beri-beri, incipient malaria, fatal asthma attacks in a hostile woodland environment. That they did not bring about my removal from camp confirmed two things for me: the unpleasantness of nature and the inefficacy of the written word, the latter a thought that keeps me humble even today.

My growing up continued in a general avoidance of the natural world as much as possible. Art history, which I pursued in undergraduate and graduate school, is an interior occupation. The only landscapes an art historian sees are those thrown on the screen in a darkened room. Instead of finishing my doctorate at Radcliffe, like others of my generation I married—in my case, a handsome Air Force pilot, and followed him across the country, an experience that introduced me to the alienation felt by pioneer women gazing at strange new landscapes that threatened and often overpowered them, which Ms. Kolodny documents so well. I did exactly the same thing they did: took plants from place to place, tried to make a garden with the plants from the last garden, tried to gentle the landscape in familiar ways.

Being married to an Air Force pilot who was often away on temporary duty or overseas, I was often left to entertain small children. At one point, when said children had just gotten out of the ankle-biter stage, we lived on a farm outside of Pocahontas, Arkansas, which had a population of 3,086, a number indelibly etched on my mind from seeing it on the sign whenever I drove into town. To pass the time, I took the girls walking in the fields of the farm on which we lived. They loved it. I loathed it. Who knew what creatures rustled in the grass? Who knew what loathsome grasshopper would land, sticky-legged, on my bare arm, and I would have to touch it to remove it? I grew paranoid watching for the cottonmouths that frequented the pond edge.

When we moved to Colorado Springs, I discovered that if I wanted to continue being a Girl Scout leader and take the troop camping, I was going to have to sleep in a sleeping bag. I cannot tell you with what reluctance I approached the first outdoor training session. It was a miserable, forgettable, underwhelming experience.

In the course of time—such is the magic of the West—we as a family acquired forty acres in the Front Range near Colorado Springs. I suffered smoke inhalation trying to cook over an open fire; had hysterics when a loon yodeled in the middle of the night; came unglued when a chipmunk jumped on top of the tent at night, certain it was a bear; and consequently refused to sleep "out." I spent the first couple of years there pruning paths so that guests could walk around the lake without getting scratched. I transplanted lilac bushes and dug holes for tulip bulbs at 8,300 feet. It takes a long time for a city girl to stop trimming paths.

In the typical progress of civilization we soon built a small cabin, walls, a roof over our heads, for it rained every afternoon in the summertime—classic city thinking. But I began looking about me, asking questions. I wrote my first book, *Beyond the Aspen Grove*, as I was learning not to trim paths. The questions I asked then are the questions I still ask now: What is living, where, and why? And if so, why so, and if not, why not? My second book, in collaboration with alpine ecologist Bette Willard, revealed to me the rigors of fieldwork in the alpine tundra, which precluded sleeping out. Fine with me. But writing a third book, this on the Green River, demanded a lot of time on river beaches.

I slept on many strands, nestled into the soft sand, lulled asleep by a rapid I had just run. In the course of writing that book I once spent three weeks on the river, with only hours off to change modes of transportation. When the end of the three weeks arrived and I didn't want to leave the river, it should have been obvious that something significant had happened to the quintessential city girl. While writing *Wind in the Rock*, I had several times walked up and down the Honnaker Trail, a path that goes from the plateau above to the San Juan River below. At the end of the writing I arranged to walk alone and to camp alone, on the beach at the edge of the river. I wrote about the sense of home given to me by a familiar ground cloth and sleeping bag, kneeling on the same rock to brush my teeth, sitting against the same tree trunk to eat my supper, being accepted by the resident collared lizard. I found the same welcome in the raw mountains of Baja California that I did on Thoreau's Assabet River in Massachusetts, poles apart in every way but one: they were the same refuge, the same habitation, the same . . . home.

Enter the reading at the University of Arizona Poetry Center. Since I had not done a reading before, I asked Lois Shelton, the wonderful woman who headed the Poetry Center, for instructions. She suggested that I find a theme in my work that would unify the passages I chose to read. That led to my going through what I had written in a concerted way for the first time. Although I occasionally use my books as reference (I tend to forget a special detail, but if I wrote it, I know where I can find it again), that's not reading, that's commerce in tidbits. I found a steady concentrated perusal of nearly twenty years of work déjà vu, a sentimental journey, nostalgia, and "Oh, my God! did I write that?" Fortunately, there were also those moments when I was glad I had written *that*.

And the theme was as startling as it was obvious: the sense of home.

Some summers ago, while working on a book on the deserts of the contiguous United States, I spent five days alone in June in the Cabeza Prieta National Wildlife Refuge, participating in a bighorn sheep count. The Cabeza Prieta lies in southernmost Arizona, on the Mexican border, beginning west of Organ Pipe National Monument and running almost to Yuma. It is an area shared with Luke Air Force Base, which uses it as a live gunnery range. Ironically, that protects the sheep, since four-wheelers do not bucket off the road and harass them, because of the danger of the unexploded ammunition that is strewn about. It is a place of bare-bones beauty, of less than three inches of rain a year, of unmitigated heat in June, the stringent edge of reasonable existence.

There, in that desert, sitting alone in a knife edge of shade, I felt more sentient than I have anywhere, any time—at home, at ease, fascinated, captivated, entranced, my eye glued to a spotting scope the metal parts of which were too hot to touch by late afternoon, my behind annealed to the chair. The miserable bee-beset blind, with a freeloading wood rat tenant in the ceiling, was home. I came back from being away from it with a sense of gladness, of recognition, of a comfortable and comforting cocoon out of which I would metamorphose. But, unlike the insect world, the memory of its confines would remain imprinted on my psyche.

Clearly home has become whatever mesquite branch I happen to hang my hat on, whatever rock is big enough to perch on, wherever I am at the moment—and that includes the Algonquin in New York or the Hyatt in Columbus, Ohio. As I have become more at home in the out-of-doors, I have become more at home in the city.

The last evening in the Cabeza Prieta, I walked up to a notch that divided the valley in which I sheep-watched from the Tule Desert to the west. I had spent the day wishing that Bill Broyles, the desert rat who had trucked Chuck Bowden and me out to our blinds, would break an axle so I could stay another few days. I still had plenty of water and plenty of food. As I made my way up the rise, I was feeling primed for the deep thoughts and rewarding insights that one is supposed to feel at the end of "profound experiences."

There must have been a Venturi effect, for the late afternoon wind burrowed through the notch and flared out downslope. I bent to walk against it, shielding my eyes against gusts of sand. The wind fretted the grasses and nudged the yuccas and shivered the paloverde branches, a rude and pushy wind.

When I reached the divide, the wind whipped my shirt and spat silt in my face. I found a big rock that was partially sheltered and upon which I could sit and survey the desert below. The wind blurred the edges of this amorphous world that lacked corners and probably went on forever, and would have forever convinced those who believed the world was flat that they were right.

What I saw was the most satisfying landscape in the world. Saguaro like green toothpicks marked the dry channels that ran down the *bajada*. At the foot of the slope all vegetation ended and left the subtle moire patterns of tans and greiges, grays and chalky whites, that can be appreciated only from a distance above. The landscape below me was the world before it was formed, the empty canvas upon which anything could be painted, the perfect landscape, flowing, uncluttered horizontals that bring a quieting of the pulse, horizontals kept from being dull by the diagonal plunge of mountains in the distance. The only one doing the painting at the moment was the wind, sanding everything down to the barest common denominator. For someone oriented to form rather than color, it was landscape at its purest and finest and most satisfying.

I sat there, content to watch the wind pluck a leaf and whirl it into patterns it had never known in life, to catch the surprise in the eye of a zebra-tailed lizard as it scampered up its rock and found me there, to feel the light dim. It occurred to me that if I wanted to get back down without being irrevocably damaged, I should go now, while the light still lasted. I thought vaguely of relying on starlight, then realized I had developed a deep sense of pragmatic conservatism living out here alone—as in "don't take stupid chances." But still I sat, purely happy, miraculously free from the necessity to think. Not until I finally picked my way down, avoiding the same spines and thorns that had showed intent to maim on the way up, did it occur to me that I had never gotten around to thinking those deep thoughts I was so culturally oriented to think.

What did occur to me was that I had survived 110-degree heat without melting, and that air-conditioning didn't seem so important anymore. I did miss ice-cold water, but realized I could get along without that, too. I had come here to work—to count sheep and to write—and I had done it to the best of my ability and felt I had used my time well. It also occurred to me that what I had gained was something more precious than introspection: the knowledge that in the desert the wind writes the laws, draws the lines, rules the world, and that I could survive for a time in that hostile world. I walked back to a familiar blue sleeping bag, having realized that while my time here was limited by physical requirements, my time in the city was limited by psychological ones.

I have come to equate "wilderness" with absolute aloneness, city with "peopleness." As isolated a profession as writing is, I don't think I could permanently live apart and remain sane enough to write—but I'm not sure of that: maybe I'd be a better writer. I know that at this time I need the city in my life, and given this time and this place, I need the combination of open spaces and city spaces. I could not exist in one without the other.

But I cannot write about the city any more than I cannot *not* write about nature. Much as the city consumes a greater part of my life as far as time goes, it does not hold the enchantment that nature does. The city does not enthrall me. Observing traffic on Speedway or Fifth Avenue is not the way I want to spend my time. Despite what the city provides, it binds and limits my horizons, and literally shuts out the horizons of open spaces.

It's hard to praise pollution or get lost in the contemplation of pavement even though a hardy dandelion and a few mosses grow valiantly between the cracks, objects worth writing about. The larger natural world offers me more images, more fascination, more challenge, more good oxygen to the head, than the city world does. Perhaps I am more at home with saguaros than I am with people. Or perhaps my focus is beyond the human world and its belief that humanity can solve all problems. It is important to me to find out—and to write about—why the spines on a saguaro are thicker on the south side of the stalk than on the north side, not why we have a national deficit. It is important to me that we all learn about the natural world, the reasonable, workable, sane, unpoliticized, not economic-theoried, uncaucused natural world. Without knowledge of the necessity of open space, its health and well-being, the structure of the entire world I know, including needful city places, is down the drain.

SUGGESTED READINGS

Kolodny, Annette. *The Land Before Her: Fantasy and Experience of the American Frontiers, 1630–1860.* Chapel Hill: University of North Carolina Press, 1984.

Zwinger, Ann. *Beyond the Aspen Grove.* Tucson: University of Arizona Press, 1970; 1988.

———. *Run, River, Run: A Naturalist's Journey Down One of the Great Rivers of the West.* Tucson: University of Arizona Press, 1975; 1984.

———. *Wind in the Rock: The Canyonlands of Southeastern Utah.* Tucson: University of Arizona Press, 1978; 1986.

———. *A Conscious Stillness.* Boston: University of Massachusetts Press, 1982; 1984.

———. *Desert Country Near the Sea: A Natural History of the Cape Region of Baja California.* Tucson: University of Arizona Press, 1984; 1987.

Zwinger, Ann, and Beatrice E. Willard. *Land Above the Trees: A Guide to American Alpine Tundra.* Tucson: University of Arizona Press, 1972; 1989.

WRITING ALONG THE EDGES

The border fence, Nogales, Sonora, 1989. (Photograph © David Burckhalter)

LUCI TAPAHONSO

Come into the Shade

I'm going to begin this presentation with my poem called "Come into the Shade."

Q: Where are you from?
A: Where I'm from is like this

        Hard summer rains
        leave hollow beads
        of moisture in the dust.

My mother says each fall:
We have to husk this corn
and throw it on top of the shed
then we'll shell it when it dries.
It's really good in the winter.

        The dogs raise a racket
        everytime someone comes home—
        it's never quiet here.
        Sometimes the chickens join in
        then the babies wake up
        wanting to play.

My father—a thin slightly
bent figure—a shovel over
his shoulder coming home

from the fields. Come into
the shade by the house.
        The Begays right up on the hill
        there had a sign last summer.
        Early in the morning, we went up
        to watch them dance.
In full view of Shiprock,
there was a drunk man dancing alone,
raising little clouds of dust in the sunlight.
        We'll just get some mutton
        at the trading post and cook it
        under the trees here.
        Let's make tortillas, too.
        And pop—regular Pepsi
        and Diet Pepsi for those on diets
        (as if it would help after eating
        ribs!)
Yippee!
Lori said when we sat down to eat.
She knows where she comes from.[1]

Lori is my elder daughter. The place that I am talking about in the poem is Shiprock, where I am from. It's in northwestern New Mexico, in the northern part of the Navajo reservation. My family has land in Shiprock. The land has been in our family for several decades now, and it's where I return, go back to. That place ensures my identity to the earth no matter where I go. How one feels about the land, how one relates to other people has a lot to do with one's religion. For myself, this has to do with the Navajo creation stories that go back to time immemorial, a time that we aren't sure of in terms of dates or of the time line. But we know that these things occurred. In the Navajo stories, there are several deities. I will concentrate on one.

The way the story goes, they said that First Man and First Woman were two of the more important deities. Most of the deities occurred in pairs or in groups, and these two were in a pair, First Man and First Woman. They said that some hunters were out (they weren't in human

74

form; they had other kinds of forms) in the surrounding area, when they came upon a small hill. It was a very clear day. This particular place is in northwest New Mexico, south of Bloomfield. There was this small cloud on top of a hill. They say the hunters were going to go over there, but they became afraid because they didn't know what it was. So they went back and told First Man and First Woman. They consulted with other deities and were told that they were the only two who could go over there. They sang several songs that were made for this particular occasion and ensured their safe trip over there. The songs ensured that whatever was there, they would be successful in meeting it and handling the situation. So they went over there, and it took a long time to get there because they had to travel a long way over a lot of hills and small rises in the desert. This is all desert area, but they went all the way over there; and in going there, they had to have certain songs to make sure they got there.

When they finally arrived there, they said they got to the top of the hill and heard a baby crying. When they got there, there were other songs that the holy people had given them, so on their approach they sang these songs. And when they got to the baby, they saw that it was a newborn baby girl. She was in human form, and that had never occurred before. This was Changing Woman. When they got there, she was wrapped in clouds. She was the first Navajo human baby, and the holy ones told First Man and First Woman that the way she was raised was going to be the way that Navajo children would be raised from then on. Many of these things are still kept today.

Changing Woman matured very quickly, and they took a lot of care to make sure that things were done correctly, that she was spoken to carefully. She learned things as she went along, the way that they wanted her to. As she grew older, she was the first one to have a puberty ceremony, called the "Kinaałdá," performed for her. When she became older, she was lonely and she wanted other people around her. There were a lot of holy people and a lot of animals and other kinds of beings, but she wanted people and she told them that. She said, "I am lonely. I really think that I want some people like me around me for companionship."

Then, after talking about it a long time, they decided that she could go ahead and do that. So she created the first four original clans from underneath each of her arms, and by rubbing the sides of her breasts she created the first four people. Each of these people was the beginning of a clan, and each of these clans was assigned an animal. An animal was assigned to each clan because the clans were in a new environment and they didn't know how to survive, so they needed the animals to serve as their guides and protectors in the world we are in now. Therefore animals and the people had a real close relationship in the beginning.

Each Navajo person has a clan. Most of these clans have to do with the land, the water, or elements of the universe. Thus, in introducing oneself you always introduce yourself by your clan. If I were at home among other Navajo people I would say, "Tódík' ǫzhí nish li." That's saying "I *am* Bitter Water," Shizhé'e Tódích'ii'nii nili. My father is Salt Water. My mother's clan is Bitter Water, and that is the same for me. But I would not say "My mother's clan is Bitter Water." I have to say "I am Bitter Water," because that's my identity. And so most people have a very strong connection to the land. The Salt Water Clan was one of the first four original clans. So my connection to the land, my connection to creation of this world and for the way I live, is directly linked to the beginning. The animal that was assigned as a guide and protector for the Salt Water Clan is the bull snake.

Most people in addition have a given name; mine is Luci Tapahonso. That is my public name. But the clan name is who I am also. My name in English is Tapahonso because that's easier to say. Most people can't say Tábaahátso. *Tábąąhá* means "beside" or "by the water," and "*tso*" means "big." So at some point when this name was given to us, maybe my relatives lived beside a lake or a large body of water. My names, both of these names, indicate water, and they both have connections with land and are crucial to my identity.

When people tell stories at home, especially the older people who aren't educated and don't use the calendar, they talk about certain things happening with elaborate descriptions of what the weather was like at that time or what the land was like, and how far they had to travel. A lot of the stories indicate distances over a wide area, mostly desert, sometimes mountains. But the weather is also very important. So the stories are very visual and very rich in imagery. For example, my mother tells the story about when my sister was born. When we were driving from Durango one evening, it was snowing and I was afraid to drive in snow; I was even more afraid because I had my parents with me, but I didn't want to let them know I was afraid. So I was real nervous about driving in the snow, and I was afraid the roads would start icing up. I was real tense, sort of praying, trying to keep from thinking that the car was going to go off the road. We were far from home, it was windy and the snow was blowing, and I thought my mother might be a little nervous about the weather. But she wasn't, because while we were driving along, she said:

> Oh, this weather just reminds me of when your little sister was born. I remember that real clearly because I went into labor early in the evening, and when we were going to the hospital, the weather was just like this. I was saying to your father, I wonder what kind of baby this is going to be—being born on a night like this. When I was in the hospital waiting for the baby, I had a bed by the window and I could hear the snow blowing against the window. When your sister was born, they didn't even have to touch her, she just started crying real loud. We were so surprised that she was just a few seconds old when she just howled out loud. They said to each other, "Well, I guess she is going to be a good singer someday because she has such a good voice."

This is the way they tell a lot of their stories. It's not important that she was born around the first of November—that wasn't really the point. The point was what the weather was like, what that had to do with my sister and the kind of person she is now. A lot of the stories deal with that. Crucial events don't occur to us by ourselves. Just because we are human and we have five senses, we think we are intelligent. We're not the only ones who notice whether people die. We're not the only ones to notice birth or tragic events or events that call for celebration. Many times the stories are told so that we realize that the land recognizes events, too. When Mount St. Helens erupted, they were saying, "I wonder who was born because that was such a great event."

I want to include this poem. It's called "A Breeze Swept Through," and it has to do with this concept of the universe that recognizes along with us events that are important.

A BREEZE SWEPT THROUGH—FOR MY DAUGHTERS

The firstborn of dawn woman slid out amid
    crimson fluid streaked with stratus clouds

        her body glistening August sunset pink
        light steam rising from her like rain on warm rocks

(a sudden cool breeze swept through the kitchen
and Grandpa smiled then sang quietly,
knowing the moment).

She came when the desert day cooled and dusk began to move in,
in that intricate changing of time she gasped and it flows

from her now with every breath with every breath.
She travels now sharing scarlet sunsets
named for wild desert flowers
her smile a blessing song.

And in mid-November, early morning darkness
after days of waiting pain the second one cried wailing.

Sucking first earth breath,
separating the heavy fog,
she cried and kicked tiny brown limbs.
Fierce movements as outside
the mist lifted as the sun is born again.
(East of Acoma, a sandstone boulder split in
two—a sharp, clean crack.)

She is born of damp mist and early sun.
She is born again woman of dawn.
She is born knowing the warm smoothness of rock.
She is born knowing her own morning strength.[2]

The ceremonies that are performed, healing ceremonies, are generally
done in the summertime. You can't tell certain stories in the wintertime
or play certain kinds of games. So activities have a lot to do with the
season. Some of the rituals were established when Changing Woman
was a baby, and this is recounted in a poem called "It Has Always Been
This Way."

Being born is not the beginning.
Life begins way before the time of birth.

Inside a mother, the baby floats in warm fluid
and the mother is careful not to go near noisy or evil places.
She will not cut meat or take part in the killing of food.
Navajo babies were always protected in this way for centuries.

The baby is born and cries out loud
and the mother murmurs and nurtures the baby.
A pinch of pollen on the baby's tongue
for strong lungs and steady growth.
The bellybutton dries and falls off
and she buries it near the house
so the child will always return home and
will always help the mother.
It has been this way for centuries among us.

The baby laughs out loud and it is celebrated—
rock salt and lots of food, relatives laughing
and passing the baby around. This is done so
the baby will always be generous, will always
be surrounded by lots of relatives.
It has been this way for centuries among us.

Much care has always been taken to shape the baby's head well,
to talk and sing to the baby softly and in the right way.
It has been this way for centuries among us.

The child starts school and leaves with a pinch of pollen
on top of the head and on the tongue.
This is so the child will think clearly,
listen quietly and learn well away from home.
The child leaves with prayers and good thoughts.
It has been this way a long time among us.

This is how you were raised.
You were raised with care and attention because
it has always been this way among us.

It has been this way for centuries among us.
This is our history and way of raising children.
It has worked well for centuries.
    You are here,
    your parents are here,
    your relatives are here,
    we are all here.

It is all this—the care, the prayers and songs
and our lives as Navajos you take with you.[3]

These things were practiced for a long time, and they were very important and guaranteed that one would return to their home. The emphasis is on family, the home, and the land. This is a philosophy that is learned early and is something that is internal and not visible. You can't tell by looking at someone how they have been raised and what they feel, what their connections are. But being raised in this way serves as one's center, and it serves as a foundation for life so that distance—where one travels, where one goes—is not really important.

Distance is important perhaps only in the convenience of renewal, of going back to renew yourself. This philosophy accepts adaptation, and it allows for change. Renewal is possible wherever there is distance and wherever there is space and land. For contemporary Navajo people who are working in the city and who come out of this background, it's a philosophy and a way of living that can be adapted wherever we move, wherever we live, because we have spent all our early years learning this and living in this way. So you adapt to the situation that you are in, and the adaptation becomes very much a contemporary sort of adaptation and it allows for change. One of the better-known clichés is that people have a really hard time adjusting, particularly Indian people, when they move to the city. You've heard the old cliché "The Indian is caught between two cultures." The "plight of the Indian" is about being unable to adjust. If one has been raised in this Navajo way, then the conflict is probably more economic than it is within oneself.

I live in Albuquerque and I work in Albuquerque because that is where my job is. There are no teaching positions on the reservation. Professionally, it is a situation that works out well. Economically, it works out well. As far as my creative work is concerned, writing poetry and being a creative writer requires solitude and space. Virginia Woolf wrote about having a room of one's own. You really do need a space just for your work, a space where you do nothing but that, where you don't change diapers, you don't balance your checkbook, or you don't do other kinds of things. It's just for your work. And for myself, that's very important.

Emotional and professional support is also very important for me. The support of my colleagues, the exchange of talking to people who are working in areas similar to my own, and being able to attend poetry readings are very important. Having access to books and research materials is necessary for me.

Had I stayed in Shiprock, I wouldn't have access to these things. We don't have a library in Shiprock. (There is one at the junior college, but it is very limited.) So facilities are very important. It's also nice to call for a pizza and have it in thirty minutes at your door. Even access to television is different. In the part of Shiprock where we live, we get only one station.

So the atmosphere and the support of my colleagues and being on a university campus are very good for my work. Intellectually I need that kind of challenge, and I need the exchange with and access to other writers. Albuquerque serves as a crossroads for the literary arts and is one of the art centers of the Southwest. This is very important.

One of the negative aspects about being in a city is that I miss my support system. I have seven sisters, and when I am in Shiprock, it is easy. There, I hardly see my children when I come home because they are off with other people. And if I don't want to cook, or if my sisters don't want to cook sometimes in the evening (which happens almost daily), we will ask, "What are you cooking? Can you bring some over here?" Or they say, "Oh, this is your busy day. I know you are tired. I have a big pot of stew and I'll bring some over and you don't have to cook." I like having help with the kids when somebody is sick, and not having to take my youngest daughter to one of the hospitals that runs an ill-children's care center—as I do in Albuquerque—so that I don't have to cancel my classes. I feel that it's just not a good situation. I'm sure you understand the guilt and apprehension from doing things like that. If I lived in Shiprock, I wouldn't have to do that. I could have her go to my mother's or my mother would come over, or one of my sisters. If my car breaks down, I end up paying mechanics' bills like other

Americans, making sure I have a car pool, and all of this. Two of my brothers are mechanics. This is their profession. If I was at home, they would do that. When I go home, they check my car and make sure everything is running right. They worry about me being in Albuquerque and not knowing anyone who's a mechanic.

Just being around my relatives is so good sometimes, to have the people come and visit me. One of my sisters lives about two hours from my mother, and she calls my mother and she says things like "Oh, nobody ever visits me. It just seems like I don't have any relatives." She can say that and my mother will say to my other relatives, "Have you been out in her area? If you are, you should just see her because she doesn't think anybody wants to visit her." And people will start visiting her, just to see how she is doing. Well, I can't say that. I can't go home to my mother and say I don't have any relatives, because I live four or five hours away from my relatives. They are rarely in my area. So I miss that connection with my relatives. Sometimes people will come over and call me, sometimes relatives I don't even know. It's very nice.

Another thing missing in my city life is accessibility to foods such as that important staple, mutton. Mutton is a Navajo delicacy. It's difficult to get good mutton in Albuquerque. We have to go to the reservation, and it's a long drive. Even the nearest reservation doesn't have it. They get theirs from Gallup. In Albuquerque, you can go to any of the grocery stores and buy what they have, but it doesn't taste right. I think they are grain-fed or they are fed differently. We like meat from animals that just roam around the desert to eat whatever they find there. That's the best kind. You can't get Navajo mutton. You can't get Navajo sheep in Albuquerque. It's also hard not being able to get the flour that you need to make fry bread. You can't use Pillsbury or anything like that. It doesn't come out right. You have to have a specific flour. These are some of the nitty-gritty difficulties of living in the city for a Navajo person.

However, people make compromises. It makes you recognize and appreciate your own beliefs and your own upbringing much more because you have to work harder at it. One of the most important things to a Navajo is to get up early and go out and pray, and your house should always face east. Sometimes that is not possible. You might get an apartment at a good rent and your door faces west. What can you do? You have to work harder at it. So you learn to accept the situation that you are in and you do the best you can, working your beliefs around it. In the end, I am grateful for the situation I am in.

You can get an idea of some of the conflict that comes up between my country and the city from what happened when they were having a Kinaaldá near the borders of the reservation. In the Kinaaldá the girl who is having the puberty ceremony has to run about two miles every morning to the east, dressed in her whole outfit: long skirt, velvet blouse, concho belt and earrings, and a lot of other jewelry. She has to run to the east and run back, and people can run after her. As she is running, she has to yell out loud to strengthen her lungs, to give her a good singing voice, so she can be physically strong. People can run after her, but they can't pass her. If they pass her, they will age before she does. And they can run after her and yell, too, because as she is running, she lets off—when people run or move quickly, they let off a breeze—that breeze is a blessing, it's a blessing for them. So that is why people run after her.

In this case they were running along the highway, and she was running ahead. I guess there weren't many girls, mainly young men and little boys were running after her. They were all running, yelling. It was a serious event, this was part of the ceremony. A state policeman came along, and he saw this. He stopped them. He thought they were trying to mug her or rob her or something. All the men were arrested. He took them all in. They finally had to tell him that this was really a legitimate event, it was just an Indian doing, and they weren't trying to harm anybody. But this gives you an idea of some of the conflicts and how people have to adapt. When the group took off running, they never came back, so the others had to go and look for them. They saw two police cars with their lights flashing, and the Indian men were sitting in the back and the young girl was sitting in the police car. They asked the police, "What did they do?" They were just supposed to run for their blessing, and they were arrested. The people had to explain the ceremony to the police.

I'm going to end with this poem. It's called "A Prayer."

This winter
I have spent many hours driving
the road between Santa Fe and Albuquerque
early morning late afternoon

It must be tiring, people say
about 100 miles a day
nothing much on that road
But I enjoy it
that road had a lot
of good poems and songs
discovered while driving
through softly curving hills
dotted with tufts of pinion and tumbleweed.
I even left some thoughts musing,
lingering around a small white cross
beside the northbound lane
and I say:

      bless me hills
      this clear golden morning
      for I am passing through again.

I can easily sing
for that time is mine
and these ragged red cliffs
flowing hills and wind echoes

      are only extensions
      of a never-ending prayer.[4]

As we drove away from Albuquerque to begin our trip to Tucson and the Open Spaces conference, the sun was still up. Hour after hour, we drove along flat desert roads, through a few low mountains and some small towns. As we traveled, my daughters and I sang with the radio, told stories, or they read books and played games. Most of the time, I thought about my presentation and composed poetry mentally.

The long stretches of highway invited this time to think, imagine, and create. The land outside my window was sparse and seemingly endless. After a normal working day in Albuquerque, how I needed and waited for that time and opportunity to drive a long distance.

As we approached Las Cruces last evening, we were relieved to see the light that meant food, watching TV, and that sign of "real" traveling—a motel room. We settled into our comfortable room for the night and savored a buffet breakfast and good coffee upon awakening. We began again to Tucson, and the drive was different this time—the changing terrain, the difference in vegetation and warmer temperatures. We realized we were outfitted for a winter that was several hundred miles north and not in Tucson.

We were excited as we came into Tucson. We liked the city immediately and set out to find our way around. We staked out museums, parks, and a McDonald's near the university area. The exploration of a new place and endless choices of food made us appreciate the long distance we traversed to get to Tucson. The city, in this instance, is a relief and a celebration of sorts after the long drive. The drive was necessary to arrive and to acknowledge the changing land and different plants, and learn new stories, songs, and poems.

Both origin point and cities merge over and over in many ways other than this. Each merging, though, can be this—celebrations and acknowledgment.

NOTES

1. Luci Tapahonso, *A Breeze Swept Through* (Albuquerque: West End Press, 1987).

2. Ibid.

3. Luci Tapahonso, "It Has Always Been This Way," in *Sáanii Dahataal/The Women Are Singing: Poems and Stories* (Tucson: University of Arizona Press, 1993), 17.

4. Luci Tapahonso, *Seasonal Woman* (Santa Fe: Tooth of Time Books, 1982).

DON GRAHAM

Land Without Myth; or, Texas and the Mystique of Nostalgia

In Texas some of us are sick of the subject of myth. That's because we are surrounded and bombarded daily with versions of a secular commercial myth, the so-called Texas mystique. In 1987 we also are recovering from having endured a yearlong celebration of the Texas sesquicentennial. Counting the buildup and the year itself, we had to put up with myth-mongering for about eighteen months. It was awful. James Michener killed whatever interest anybody might have been able to summon forth when he jumped the gun and published his doorstop of a novel even before the calendar year 1986 began. And the slump in oil prices killed a little interest, too.

The only stimulating thing about the sesquicentennial was its ironic timing—it came right in the middle of the decline of oil prices. So instead of celebrating the rich panoramas of the past, some of the rich spent much of 1986 hiding out on their ranches and attending auctions; only they weren't buying, they were selling.

Still, there were a few lame attempts at celebration, self-evaluation, and the sort of backward glances that are supposed to accompany events such as a 150-year milestone. A television station in Corpus Christi mounted a PBS-style documentary called *Lone Star*. It recycled all the old myths: Texans are strong, Texans are independent, Texans are blah, blah, blah. Meanwhile, every oilman in Texas was looking to the federal government to bail him out. Jimmy Dean, the mythic sausage maker, squinted into the camera and said, "Ah know the meaning of temporary setback, but Ah don't know the meaning of defeat." Larry

Hagman, dressed as J. R. Ewing, introduced the show, with a Texas flag waving in the landward breezes wafting across his adobe palace. The *merde* in *Lone Star* was deeper than the sand at Malibu.

All through 1986 the myth was showing signs of strain. A wagon train with a bunch of pioneer-style senior citizens, early retirees dressed up in leggings and calico, was supposed to travel all around the state, but by early spring they were out of money and nobody gave a damn.

In a modest way, all through the eighties I've been writing about Texas's propensity to advertise itself at the expense of facts. In three books, one about movies, one about literature, and one that was literature—an anthology that I edited of modern Texas short stories in a realistic vein—I depicted a Texas a little different from the one celebrated in film, song, and beer commercials.[1] What I quickly learned, though, was that the media preferred the stereotypes. At various times I was interviewed by the national media—by CBS during the Republican convention in Dallas in 1984, for example, and by *USA Today*. I'd answer their questions as truthfully as I could, and then they'd edit my answers to fit their needs. As a result I always come out sounding like (1) a fatuous spokesman for the Sweetwater Chamber of Commerce or (2) a fatuous spokesman for the Republican party.

My message is simple. Texas is a land largely without a "land myth." In modern Texas, where I live, the land is almost wholly given over to malls. What hasn't been malled or condoed o'er awaits the next boom. Then we'll finish paving the rest of the state that's inhabitable.

Needless to say, I don't own a foot of land. I'm afraid if I did, I'd start writing like John Graves, one of the state's most treasured writers. Graves is a landowner who feels compelled to write about it. He won't let anybody alone about his land; it's his only subject, and has been for nearly thirty years. Herewith, a typical passage from one of his books:

> . . . inside me somewhere there has always been the incipient disease of the land. . . . I had never managed to purge myself of the simple yeoman notion, contracted in childhood from kinsmen looking back to a rural past, that grass and crops and trees and livestock and wild things and water mattered somehow supremely, that you were not whole unless you had a stake in them, a daily knowledge of them.[2]

Anytime somebody calls himself a "simple yeoman," you know you are listening to a landowner and not to a simple yeoman. I guess if you own land, it means something to you. Not being given to mysticism—my forebears had all of that stamped out of them when they stopped being Catholics and started being Protestants on the way to being Nothing—I would have to say, in the lingo of the region, land don't mean much to me in and of itself.

The most land in Texas is in West Texas, if you are talking about empty land, and I wouldn't give a dime for most of it. Oh, the Big Bend country has its pleasures, and the Palo Duro Canyon is very fine, but the land around Midland, Odessa, Abilene, Lubbock? Recently I flew over West Texas in a small plane, and a historian on the trip with me, looking down on that vast and thinly populated flatness, said he figured if the water gave out like the oil had, and all the kids kept moving to Dallas or Houston, which they have been doing pretty steadily since World War II, then in the future West Texas might become like the Australian outback—desolate, which it already is, and empty, which it almost is. (Except at night. At night West Texas is amazingly aglow with electric lights. From Abilene to Austin there's a solid connecting grid of lights on the land—very strange.)

So I think the only people who care about land in Texas are those who own some. It helps if you own a ranch and have read J. Frank Dobie. Unfortunately, I grew up on a cotton farm in north central Texas, in Collin County, three miles from where TV's Southfork is located. Talk about myth! There weren't any cowboys in my part of Texas when I was growing up. All the cowboys were in Fort Worth at the Fat Stock Show or at the Texas Theatre in McKinney, where Gene Autry and Roy Rogers and Sunset Carson rode amid snow-clad mountains just north of Galveston in pursuit of justice and demure brunettes. The Western had everything going for it—grandeur, horses, heroes. Cotton country had heat, starve-out farms, mules, and guys who dressed like Tom Joad. There never was a genre called the sharecropper movie.

So I came from cotton farming country and wanted out of it as quick as I could. Maybe if my dad had owned several counties and had a big plantation house, I'd have liked the cotton way of life. But he didn't, and I didn't. So I became a professor and now find myself, again and again, talking about land and landscapes—literary landscapes.

The land in Texas literature acquires what force it does for me through ironic portraits of space and, conversely, limitations.

Larry McMurtry, the best-known Texas writer since Dobie, has a nice ironic touch when he writes about the land. In his first novel, *Horseman, Pass By*, there is a fine moment that shows what I mean. The boy Lonnie is dreaming, and in his dream he and his grandfather, a throwback to the old wild days, sit on their horses on a ledge overlooking some rolling country. McMurtry writes, "There below us was Texas, green and brown and graying in the sun, spread wide under the clear spread of sky like the opening scene in a big Western movie."[3]

Notice how the Western movie reference frames the scene. What would have been nostalgia is undercut just enough. The country is beautiful in a minimalist sort of way, but it's seen through the controlling, ironic lens of a movie; also, it's a dream. In McMurtry's novel *Texasville*, there's a very funny bit of landscape description that shows he can still work that side of the street. He's describing the results of a boomlet in his favorite West Texas town: "Across the street were the new municipal tennis courts, the latest addition to the Thalia skyline. The west edge of town was so flat and ugly that a tennis net could legitimately count as an addition to the skyline."[4] Yet, as McMurtry knows better than anybody, what readers want most is not the real landscape but dreamscape; that's why his best-selling book—indeed, his only book that has sold really well—is *Lonesome Dove*, a novel set in the nineteenth century, at a time before there were fences, oilmen, or high-rises.

Dobie, McMurtry's famous predecessor and still much beloved by many Texans, wrote only about the landscape of nostalgia, and he believed it would never end. That's why among older readers in Texas, Dobie remains popular and why all of his books are in print. Here is Dobie celebrating the place where he was raised:

> No matter what is discontinued, the land remains. A thousand years, ten thousand years hence, the Dobie ranch will be where it was before the Ramirez Grant took in a portion of its pristine acreage. It will have other names, be divided and then be absorbed. The land will always be grazing land, for neither soil nor climate will permit it to be anything else.[5]

In less romantic terms, what Dobie is really saying is that the land is so sorry, it will escape all the ravages of possible change and transformation. It will endure because it is so sorry. (Do you know the word "sorry"? In Texas that means "worthless." It's what you say about something or somebody that's no good.)

John Houghton Allen, whose 1952 book *Southwest* ought to be better known than it is, has a fine description of sorry country: "For this is hard country, brush country, mean country, heartbreak country. Ugly in summer, drought-stricken, dusty, glaring, but in winter it is hideous."[6] He was talking about South Texas, but I think he meant most of the state. He said all you could do in such country was drink and fornicate.

Richard Harding Davis, that intrepid reporter-adventurer, now largely forgotten, viewed Texas from the window of a train car on his trip to the West in 1891. South Texas, along the border, he called the "backyard of the world"—a country, he said, "where there are no roses, but where everything that grows has thorn."[7] These observations inevitably bring to mind what General Phil Sheridan said about Texas: "If I owned Hell and Texas, I'd rent out Texas and live in Hèll."

Land so desolate, so empty, has provoked a kind of wonder in some writers. One is Loula Grace Erdman, whose novel *The Edge of Time* (1950) evokes all those moments, in Western and in Texas literature, when a woman from a more sheltered environment confronts her fate—displacement and disorientation—usually because of a marriage.

> The first thing Bethany saw was nothing. Nothing at all. She pitched her mind in nothingness, found herself drowning in it as a swimmer drowns in water too deep for him.
>
> Here was more sky than she had ever seen before. That was all there was—sky. No houses, no trees, no roads. Nothing to break the landscape. She shrank back from it as one draws back from sudden bright light.
>
> "Aren't there—aren't there any *trees*?" she asked Wade.
>
> "Not on the high plains. Too dry for them. They grow down in the breaks though."
>
> She thought she could not bear a place without trees. They broke up nothingness. They cut a land down to something you could stand to contemplate.[8]

This same Panhandle landscape—or skyscape, one might better call it—inspired some of Georgia O'Keeffe's most daring early work. And that painterly writer Gertrude Stein, on a 1937 swing through the state, put it this way:

> Texas is a level surface. . . . We saw the flatland and we saw the cattle not so many of them it had been a bad year for cattle as there had been too much cold weather and too much dry weather and as they do not in any way protect them they all died not all of them but a lot of them still it was a pleasure to see them and even see some cowboys and one cowgirl go toward them.[9]

Stein saw the level surface of Texas from an automobile window, and that's the way most Texans relate to the land—by driving across it as fast as they can.

So Texas, I insist, has no land myth that empowers or nourishes its devotees. In Texas the "remembered earth" is the land the family sold to make a killing on, or is the property used to hunt deer on, or is something one wished to escape from because it was so harsh and unforgiving. Myth in Texas is either (a) a system of belief in profits, development, and expansion that is commercially defined and perpetuated through advertising, self-promotion, and schools of business, or (b) a monolithic Anglo interpretation of the past in which everything begins at the Alamo and ends at Southfork; or (c) an anti-myth in which the world, to use Mircea Eliade's terms, is profane rather than sacred. I don't think eighty-two percent of Texans, the figure that currently lives in cities, spend much time at all remembering the earth. Perhaps they should, but they don't.

History, in Texas anyway, is on their side. There is no model in Anglo Texas culture for thinking about Mother Earth. Early on, Indians in Texas were killed or driven out of the state, so that in contrast, say, with New Mexico, there was never in Texas a civilization of Indian culture approaching the complexity and richness of Pueblo culture in New Mexico.

But I'm always reluctant to generalize too much about such matters. What I want to suggest instead is a point about the selectivity of all myths, all systems that are designed to transmit a structure of beliefs and values from the past to the present. Mythmaking is a very selective process, and if you are looking for Indians to emulate, I offer the following negative model, from Cabeza de Vaca's great narrative, the first Southwestern prose work of art. (I quote from the English translation by Cyclone Covey, *Adventures in the Unknown Interior of America*.) De Vaca is describing the quaint practices of some people he called the Mariames, whom he encountered in Texas sometime around 1535.

> They cast away their daughters at birth; the dogs eat them. They say they do this because all the nations of the region are their enemies, whom they war with ceaselessly; and that if they were to marry off their daughters, the daughters would multiply their enemies until the latter overcame and enslaved the Mariames, who thus preferred to annihilate all daughters [rather] than risk their reproduction of a single enemy. We asked why they them-

selves did not marry these girls. They said that marrying relatives would be a disgusting thing. It was better to kill them than to give them to either kin or foe.[10]

These are not exactly Willa Cather Indians, are they? Their "lifestyle" is a little chilling, don't you think? This bit of amateur anthropology on De Vaca's part serves to remind us that in all times and all places there may be forms of behavior that seem, how shall I put it, less than liberal humanistic.

The absence of an Indian presence in Anglo Texas is, then, one of the possible sources of the missing mysticism about the land. What about the Hispanics? There, too, it seems to me, Texas is fundamentally different from other, more exotic Southwestern states. Texas Hispanic writers such as Tomás Rivera and Rolando Hinojosa have as little mysticism in their works as any of the Texas Anglo writers, which is to say none at all. I can't explain why, except perhaps that in Texas, unlike New Mexico, for example, where several cultures coexist on their own autonomous terms, in Texas the Anglo commercial view has dominated to an extraordinary degree. And that view holds that land is personal property and not the sacred body of Mother Earth. Those of us who live in cities and own no land, I repeat, spend very little time thinking about land. And never mystically.

In modern Texas, the ideal is Las Colinas, an upscale mixed residence/business development on what was once raw prairie just north of Dallas, near the Dallas-Fort Worth Airport. Las Colinas is a twenty-first-century suburb, intones an article in *USA Today*. And in a post-modernist description worthy of Donald Barthelme, we learn that "a third of Las Colinas is open space. Flowers are changed five times yearly." In Texas, land—and its corollary, nature—must be shaped to capitalism's needs.

NOTES

1. Don Graham, *Cowboys and Cadillacs: How Hollywood Looks at Texas* (Austin: Texas Monthly Press, 1983); *Texas: A Literary Portrait* (San Antonio, Tex.: Corona, 1985); and (ed.) *South by Southwest: 24 Stories from Modern Texas* (Austin: University of Texas Press, 1986).

2. John Graves, *Hard Scrabble: Observations on a Patch of Land* (New York: Alfred A. Knopf, 1974), 42.

Don Graham

3. Larry McMurtry, *Horseman, Pass By* (New York: Penguin, 1961, 1979), 60.

4. Larry McMurtry, *Texasville* (New York: Simon and Schuster, 1987), 32.

5. J. Frank Dobie, *Some Part of Myself* (Boston: Little, Brown, 1967), 33.

6. John Houghton Allen, *Southwest* (Albuquerque: University of New Mexico Press, 1952, 1977), 9.

7. Richard Harding Davis, *The West from a Car-Window* (New York: Harper & Brothers, 1892), 41, 42.

8. Loula Grace Erdman, *The Edge of Time* (New York: Dodd, Mead, 1950), 53.

9. Gertrude Stein, *Everybody's Autobiography* (New York: Random House, 1937), 274, 275.

10. Cabeza de Vaca, *Adventures in the Unknown Interior of America*, trans. Cyclone Covey (Albuquerque: University of New Mexico Press, 1983), 78.

94

ROLANDO HINOJOSA-SMITH

The Texas-Mexico Border: This Writer's Sense of Place

I find it appropriate that a paper on borders should begin with a quote from a Borderer, in this case, from a man imprisoned for his participation in the Texas-Santa Fe expedition of 1841. While in his cell in Mexico City, he spurned Santa Anna's offer of freedom in exchange for renouncing the Republic of Texas. Those words of 1842 were said by a man who had signed the Texas Declaration of Independence and who had served in the Congress of the Republic. Later, he cast a delegate vote for annexation and contributed to the writing of the first state constitution. He won election to the state legislature and still later he supported secession. And this is what he said:

> I have sworn to be a good Texan; and that I will not forswear. I will die for that which I firmly believe, for I know it is just and right. One life is a small price for a cause so great. As I fought, so shall I be willing to die. I will never forsake Texas and her cause. I am her son.[1]

The words were written by José Antonio Navarro, a Texan, and thus a native of a state that borders four states of the Union and shares an 800-mile border with Mexico. He knew that last border well. I count myself fortunate to have been born and raised as a Borderer, for it has given me what I call a sense of place: in my case, the Lower Rio Grande Valley of Texas.

The year 1983 marked the centennial of the birth of my father, Manuel Guzmán Hinojosa, on the Campacuás Ranch, some four miles north of the Rio Grande; his father was born on that ranch, as was his father's father. My mother arrived in the valley at the age of six weeks in the year 1887, among the first Anglo American settlers enticed by Jim Wells, one of the early developers of the northern bank. It's no accident that Jim Wells County in South Texas is named for him.

One of the earliest stories I heard about Grandfather Smith was a supposed conversation he held with lawyer Wells. You are being asked to imagine the month of July 1887 in the valley, with no air-conditioning. Wells was extolling the valley, and said that all it needed was a little water and a few good people. My grandfather replied, "Well, that's all Hell needs, too." The story is apocryphal—it has to be; but living in the valley, and hearing that type of story, laid the foundation for what I later learned was to give me a sense of place. By that I do not mean that I had a feel for the place; no, not at all. I had a sense of it, and by that I mean that I was not learning about the culture of the border but living it, forming part of it, and thus contributing to it.

A place is merely that until it is populated, and once populated, the histories of the place and its people begin. For me and mine, history began in 1749, when the first colonists began moving to the southern and northern banks of the Rio Grande. That river was not yet a jurisdictional barrier and would not be until almost one hundred years later; but by then, the border had its own history, its own culture, and its own sense of place: it was Nuevo Santander, named for old Santander in the Spanish Peninsula.

The last names were similar up and down on both banks of the river, and as second and third cousins were allowed to marry, this further promulgated and propagated blood relationships and that sense of belonging that led the Borderers to label their fellow Mexicans who came from the interior *fuereños*, or outsiders. And later, when *la gente del norte*—the people from the north—started coming to the border, they were labeled *gringos*, a word meaning "foreigner" and nothing else until the *gringos* themselves, from all evidence, took the term as a pejorative label.

For me, then, part of a sense of the border came from sharing; the sharing of names, of places, of a common history, a common lore, and of belonging to the place. One attended funerals, was taken to cemeteries, and saw names that corresponded to one's own or to one's friends and neighbors and relatives.

When I first started to write and being what we call *empapado*—

which translates as "drenched," "soaked," or "drunk"—with the place, I had to eschew the romanticism and the sentimentalism that tend to blind the unwary, that get in the way of truth. It's no great revelation that romanticism and sentimentalism tend to corrupt clear thinking as well. The border wasn't paradise, and it didn't have to be; for it was more than paradise—it was home. And as Robert Frost once wrote, "Home, when you have to go there, is the place where they have to take you in."

And the border was home. It was also the home of the petty office-holder elected by an uninformed citizenry; a home for bossism, and for smuggling as a way of life for some. But it also maintained the remains of a social democracy that cried out for independence, for a desire to be left alone, and for the continuity of a sense of community.

The history one learned there was an oral one and somewhat akin to the oral religion brought by the original colonials. Many of my generation were raised with the music written and composed by valley people, and we learned the ballads of the border, little knowing that it was a true native art form. And one was also raised and steeped in the stories and exploits of Juan Nepomuceno Cortina in the nineteenth century, and with stories of the Texas Rangers in that century and other Ranger stories in this century. And, as always, names, familiar patronymics: Jacinto Treviño, Aniceto Pizaña, the Seditionists of 1915 who had camped in Mercedes; my father would take me and show and mark for me the spot where the Seditionists had camped and barbecued their meat half a generation before. These were men of flesh and bone who lived and died there in Mercedes, in the valley. And then there were the stories of the Revolution of 1910, and of the participation in it for the next ten years off and on by valley *mexicanos*—Borderers—who fought alongside their south bank relatives. And the stories told to me and to those of my generation by exiles, men and women from Mexico who earned a living by teaching school on the northern bank while they bided their time to return to Mexico.

But we didn't return to Mexico; we didn't have to. We were Borderers with a living and unifying culture born of conflict with another culture. This, too, helped to cement further still the knowledge of exactly where one came from and from whom one was descended.

The language also was a unifier and as strong an element as there is in fixing one's sense of place. The language of the border is a derivative of the Spanish language of northern Mexico, a language in which some nouns and other grammatical elements are forms no longer used in the Spanish Peninsula but persist there. The more the linguistically uninformed went out of their way to denigrate the language, the stiffer the resistance to maintain it and to nurture it on the northern bank. And the uninformed failed, of course, for theirs was a momentary diversion while one was committed to its preservation; the price that many Texas Mexicans paid for keeping the language and the sense of place has been exorbitant.

As Borderers, the north bank Mexicans couldn't, to repeat a popular phrase, "go back to where they came from." The Borderers were there and had been there before the interlopers; but what of the indigenous population prior to the 1749 settlement? Since Nuevo Santander was never under the presidio system and since its citizens did not build missions that trapped and stultified the indigenous people, the latter remained there and, in time, settled down or were absorbed by the colonial population. Thus the phrase hurled at the border Mexican, "Go back where you came from," was, to use another popular term, "inoperative." And this, too, fostered that sense of place.

For the writer—this writer—a sense of place was not just a matter of importance; it became essential. And so much so, that my stories are not held together by the peripeteia, or the plot, as much as by *what* the people who populate the stories say and *how* they say it; how they look at the world out and at the world in. My works, then, become studies of perceptions and values and decisions reached by them because those perceptions and values were fashioned and forged by the place and its history.

What I am saying here is not to be taken to mean that it is impossible for a writer to write about a place, its history, and its people if the writer is not from that particular place; it can be done, and it has been done. What I *am* saying is that I needed a sense of place, and that this helped me no end in the way that Américo Paredes in *With His Pistol in His Hand* and Tomás Rivera in . . . *and the Earth Did Not Part* were helped by a sense of place, the Texas-Mexico border. And I say this because to me, these writers and others like them impart a sense of place and a sense of truth about the place and about the values of that place. It isn't a studied attitude but, rather, one of a certain love, and an understanding of the place that they captured in print for themselves: something that was, for them, at that time and that place.

A sense of place for Philip Roth is Newark, New Jersey, a marginalized border city. Thus we see him surprised at himself when he crosses the border, dates a *schicksa*, and then, wonderful storyteller that he is, tells us of his Jewish traditions and conflicts. Another border, this one, but a border still; and one notes that these border conflicts become a pattern in some of Roth's writings whenever he writes of relationships—which, after all, is what writers usually write about.

I am not making a medieval pitch for the shoemaker to stick to his last, but if a writer places a lifetime of living in a work, he or she sometimes finds it difficult to remove the place of provenance from the writings, irrespective of where the stories are situated. That's a strong statement, and one that may elicit comment or disagreement; but what spine one has is formed early in life, and it is formed at a specific place. Later on, when one grows up, one may mythicize, adopt a persona, become an actor, restructure family history; but the original facts of one's formation remain, as facts always do.

It's a personal thing, because I found that after many years of hesitancy, and fits and spurts and false starts, that despite what education I had acquired, I was still limited in many ways. Whatever I attempted to write came out false and frail. I know I wanted to write, had to write, was burning to write, and all of those things that some writers say to some garden clubs; but the truth and heart of the matter was that I did not know where to begin. There it was again, that adverb of place, the *where*. And then I got lucky: I decided to write whatever it was I had in Spanish, and I decided to set it on the border, in the valley. As reduced as that space was, it was Texas with all its contradictions and its often repeated, one-sided telling of Texas history. When the characters stayed in the Spanish-speaking milieu or society, the Spanish language worked well.

It was in the natural order of things that English made its entrance when the characters strayed or found themselves in Anglo institutions. In cases where the two cultures came into contact, both languages were used, and where one and only one would do, I would follow that dictate as well. What dominated at first, then, was the place. Later I discovered that generational and class differences also dictated not only usage but also *which* language. From this came *how* they said *what* they said.

As the census rolls filled up in the works, so did some distinguishing features, characteristics, viewpoints, values, decisions. Thus I used the valley and the border, *and* the history of the people. The freedom to do this led me to use the folklore and the anthropology of the border, and whatever literary form I desired and saw fit to use to tell my stories: dialogues, duologues, monologues, imaginary newspaper clippings, and whatever else I felt would be of use. And it *was* the border, the valley, but it remained forever Texas. At the same time, I could see this valley, this border, and I drew a map. This, too, was another key, and led to more work and to more characters in that place.

It was a matter of luck in some ways, as I said, but mostly it was the proper historical moment. I took what had been there for some time, but that I had not been able to see, since I had not fully developed a sense of place. I had left the border for the military service, for formal university training, and for a series of very odd jobs, only to return to it in my writing.

I've mentioned values and decisions; as I see them, these are matters inculcated by one's elders first, by one's acquaintances later on, and usually under the influence of one's society, which is another way of saying one's place of origin. Genetic structure may enter into holding certain values and perhaps the manner of reaching decisions, for all I know. Ortega y Gasset, among others, I suspect, wrote that people make dozens of decisions every day, and that the process helps them to make and to reach more serious, deliberate, and even important decisions when the time presents itself. A preparatory stage, as it were. The point of this is that my decision to write what I write and where I choose to situate the writing is not based on anything other than the decision to write about what I know, the place I know, the language used, the values held. When someone mentions universality, I say that what happens to my characters happens to other people at given times, and I've no doubt on that score.

What also has helped me to write has been a certain amount of questionable self-education, a long and fairly misspent youth in the eyes of some, an acceptance of certain facts and some misrepresentations of the past I could change, that led to a rejection not of those unalterable facts but of hypocrisy and the smugness of the self-satisfied. For this and other personal reasons, humor creeps into my writing once in a while, because it was the use of irony that allowed the Borderer to survive and to maintain a certain measure of dignity.

Serious writing is deliberate as well as a consequence of arriving at a decision. What one does with it may be of value or not, but I believe that one's fidelity to history is the first step in fixing a sense of place, whether that place is a worldwide arena or a corner of it, as mine is—the Texas-Mexico border.

NOTES

1. James A. Wilson, *Tejanos, Chicanos, and Mexicanos: A Partially Annotated, Historical Bibliography for Texas Public School Teachers* (San Marcos: Southwest Texas State University, 1974), iii.

TOM MILLER

Brits, Beats, and the Border: A Reader's Guide to Border Travels

The image that the U.S.-Mexico borders gets from afar is very different from the way we look at it from a distance of sixty miles. Whether you grew up in the Midwest or on the East Coast, or even in the interior of Mexico, your perceptions of the borderland are based not on firsthand observation or secondhand rumors, but on books, movies, television, and music. I first heard of border towns through the song "The Streets of Laredo." Not knowing where Laredo was, or what white linen felt like, I simply knew at age three, in Washington, D.C., that the fate of the border town cowboy sounded both romantic and sad.

I moved to Arizona in the late 1960s, and very shortly afterward I went camping with some friends in an area near a ghost town named Ruby, northwest of Nogales in an area called California Gulch. We came across some twisted barbed wire lying on the ground. I stepped over it, and someone in the group said, "By the way, you're in Mexico now."

"Really?" I replied, and I stepped back into the United States. Then I started jumping back and forth, sort of like jump rope. There was something about the joyful anarchy of defying an international border by hopping two feet forward and backward that appealed mightily to me. I inhaled it, and I still have it within me. When I am at other spots along the U.S.-Mexico border, or at other international boundaries, I still remember that initial experience and I still retain that giggle.

The image that many of us get of the border towns from a distance is that they are sleepy, sleazy, dusty, and dirty. The writers among us bring passion to the border. We romanticize it. Occasionally we bring stereotypes to it, and often rather condescending ones at that. We exaggerate it. We illuminate it. We find it sexy. We find it depressing, hypnotic, magical, mysterious. We find it resilient and self-reliant. We find it a place where innocence comes from hedonism. Dollars turn into pesos. Humans become illegals. It's used as a metaphor for the human experience. The border is a painfully real place and a very symbolic one as well.

After my initial trip in 1978 along the full length of the border, from the Gulf of Mexico to the Pacific Ocean, I came to a conclusion that had started out as a premise: that the border is a third country, two thousand miles long and twenty miles wide, a nation with its own music, its own food, its own laws, and its own outlaws. It has its own politics and its own policymakers. Certainly it has its own economic system. The people on both sides of the border have far more in common with each other than they do with those in the interior of their own countries.

I have, on occasion, presented this notion in public gatherings, and it has achieved a certain degree of acceptance. It certainly didn't originate with me. A while back I presented this idea on a panel that included Jorge Bustamante, the outstanding Mexican scholar on affairs of the border. He tore it to shreds. He didn't like it at all. He mocked it. He was derisive. My respect for him plummeted. He maintained that to posit the concept of a "third country" is to advance another example of cultural imperialism, so that it allows the United States to expand another ten miles into Mexico. The border is absolute, he said. There are so many more differences than similarities that the idea is nothing more than a superficial and romanticized look at the border.

The idea of a "third country" is a notion that I continue to present. Circumstances have changed what goes on along the border a fair amount. When I first crossed the line, the peso was worth a peso, and people came and went in a routine established generations earlier. The symbiosis has changed somewhat, and the contours of the borderland have been altered as well; but despite the convolutions, the land between the United States and Mexico still retains the laissez-faire characteristics of a colony ruled from two faraway capitals.

About the same time the Instituto Nacional de Bellas Artes in Mexico held a *mesa redonda* discussion of border literature in Mexico City. The panelists consisted of five Mexicans and five participants from the United States. Of those five, I was the one gringo. Nine of the ten discussed border literature and offered a class analysis. They talked about it in Marxist terms. Their criteria for judging literature of the borderland included social strata, education level, and even health care—all the social science characteristics. I was alone in describing the border and the literature it provokes as having that tug-on-the-sleeve lure. This romanticized picture that I presented in Mexico City evolved partly from growing up far from the border. I got trounced again.

When I present the idea of writing about the American Southwest or the countries south of it to book and magazine editors in New York, the first thing they do is to quote this maxim attributed to James Reston: "People are willing to do anything for Latin America except read about it." Then, having established the balance of power in our discussions, they entertain my proposals. On one occasion in the early 1970s, an editor at *Esquire* called from New York, described an event that was about to take place in Houston, and asked if I would—I believe these were his exact words—amble on over there and cover it for them. I informed him that if we both started at the same time, he in New York and I in Arizona, he would amble into Houston before me.

For *On the Border* I had an editor who alternately exasperated me and left me in admiration. I can pinpoint one of the reasons for the former. I was in his office going over the manuscript, and he got to the chapter about Columbus, New Mexico. "Now," said my editor, "about this guy Pancho Villa"—he said it to rhyme with "ranch-oh killuh." I winced. Eventually I came to appreciate him for the very same reason. His absolute ignorance about the Southwest, his total lack of knowledge about the borderland, worked well for my manuscript and the book it finally became. He had a strong intellectual curiosity and was willing to be informed and convinced, despite his horrendous pronunciation. If I could win him over, I could feel more assured of the book's acceptability among the vast majority of Americans who have only distant impressions of the borderland.

The quote from James Reston, coupled with my editor's curiosity, brings to mind the enormous breakthrough made by Alan Riding's book about Mexico, *Distant Neighbors*. It actually made the best-seller list for a number of weeks. This was the first time a nonfiction book about contemporary Mexico—or almost anything in Latin America—

had achieved that level of popularity. For this book to fracture the conventional wisdom dictating that nonfiction books on Latin America can't sell well was a remarkable advance.

Many people get their image of the border from songs—I think here particularly of the Marty Robbins cowboy classic, "El Paso." It lends itself greatly to the image of the border. Not only is it stellar within its genre, but it's of a certain breed in which the Anglo singer falls in love with the Mexican woman. Throughout country and western music, and to a lesser extent rock and roll, you find lyrics about a gringo who is down and out, who goes to a bar along the border and sees a flirtatious Chicana or Mexicana. Of course this woman has beautiful eyes and wears a peasant blouse and often a wide embroidered skirt, and she falls for him. Usually there is a shoot-out or some twist at the end that seals the two into eternal longing. Not once have I ever heard a song from the Mexican woman's point of view, about falling in love with a gringo. Neither the image nor the reality lends itself to balladry.

If you were rich and you wanted a divorce in the 1950s, like the Rockefellers, you went to Nevada. But if you didn't have much money, you headed for the border—Juárez in particular. A friend told me that when she was seven years old her mother went to Juárez for a few days. "And when she returned, she had a black lace mantilla for me and a divorce for herself." That was her first impression of the border.

If you look at newspapers in El Paso and Juárez from that era, you see advertisements for divorce brokers. They would fix you up with a lawyer, find a decent hotel for you, and somebody would run up to your room and you would sign a few papers. After forty-eight or seventy-two hours you had a Mexican divorce. It was a cottage industry in Juárez, and to a lesser extent in other towns along the border.

In 1950, the bard of Paterson, New Jersey, William Carlos Williams, had just finished a speaking tour of California and was headed east by train. He stopped in El Paso to visit some friends. When out-of-towners stop in El Paso for a day, they always get taken across to Juárez for the evening, and Williams's visit was no exception. Williams was a sophisticated fellow, but he had never traveled in a land like Mexico.

Here we have Dr. Williams, at age sixty-seven, going for the first time into the Third World. His buddies just walk around what looked like a pile of rags. Williams is mortified because it isn't a pile of rags—there's

a body in there! This becomes so unnerving that he starts to question
his own identity. What is he—is he a poet? What is this blob in the middle of the bridge? Williams was so shaken by this and subsequent impressions that evening, that he put them to verse and came up with the
poem "The Desert Music," bits of which follow:

> —the dance begins: to end about a form
> propped motionless—on the bridge
> between Juarez and El Paso—unrecognizable
> in the semi-dark
>
>   Wait!
>
> the others waited while you inspected it,
> on the very walk itself
>
>   Is it alive?
>
>   —neither a head,
>
> legs nor arms!
>
>   It isn't a sack of rags someone
> has abandoned here   .   torpid against
> the flange of the supporting girder   .   ?
>
>   . . .
>
>   What a place to sleep!
> on the International Boundary. Where else,
> interjurisdictional, not to be disturbed? . . .
>
>   —it looks too small for a man.
> A woman. Or a very shriveled old man.
> Maybe dead. They probably inspect the place
> and will cart it away later   .
>
>   Heave it into the river. . . .

Williams is out on the streets of Juárez, and he's mesmerized by everything he sees—there's a sense of revulsion in it, but he's fascinated as

well. He and his friends have had a few drinks, and they're simply
walking along, watching people sell food and other items from booths.

> . . . the pressure moves from booth to booth
> along the curb. Opposite, no less insistent
> the better stores are wide open. Come in
> and look around. You don't have to buy: hats,
> riding boots, blankets
>
>   Look at the way,
> slung from her neck with a shawl, that young
> Indian woman carries her baby!
>
>   —a stream of Spanish,
>
> as she brushes by, intense, wide-
> eyed in eager talk with her boy husband
>
> —three half-grown girls, one of them eating a
> pomegranate. Laughing.
>
>   and a serious tourist,
> man and wife, middle-aged, middle-western,
> their arms loaded with loot, whispering
> together—still looking for bargains
>
>   and the aniline
> red and green candy at the little booth
> tended by the old Indian woman.
>   Do you suppose anyone actually
> buys—and eats the stuff? . . .

Williams goes to more booths, where he finds the Indians and Mexicans talking and singing.

> Why don't these Indians get over this nauseating
> prattle about their souls and their loves and sing
> us something else for a change? . . .

In the street it hit
me in the face as we started to walk again. Or
am I merely playing the poet? Do I merely invent
it out of whole cloth? I thought   .

What in the form of an old whore in
a cheap Mexican Joint in Juarez, her bare
buttocks waggling crazily can be
so refreshing to me, raise to my ear
so sweet a tune, built of such slime? . . .

So this is William
Carlos Williams, the poet . . . .[1]

Rather than hide or sublimate this crisis of identity provoked by the border town scene he had experienced, Williams turned it into the poem I've just radically compressed, and delivered it to the Phi Beta Kappa chapter at Harvard University.

There is a certain romance, a certain harshness to the border that many travel writers bring with them. The British love to write about the border and the Third World in general. It makes them feel so imperial. In *Another Mexico*, Graham Greene wrote:

> Over there everything is going to be different. Life is never going to be quite the same after your passport has been stamped and you find yourself speechless among the money changers. The man seeking scenery imagines strange woods and unheard of mountains; the romantic believes that the women over the border will be more beautiful and complaisant than those at home; the unhappy man imagines at least a different hell; the suicidal traveler expects the death he never finds. The atmosphere of the border—it is like starting over again; there is something about it like a good confession; poised for a few happy moments between sin and sin. When people die on the border they call it "a happy death."[2]

The first official writings about the border were the journals of the first two border survey commissioners on the U.S. side, William Emory and John Russell Bartlett, one written in the 1840s and the other in the 1850s. Bartlett was more the writer and less the surveyor; Emory was less of a writer and more of a surveyor. But the three volumes that

Emory left of his survey of the border were illustrated with beautiful color plates of some of the flora and fauna he encountered.

In 1909, an adventurer named William Hornaday started out in Tucson with some other scientists and went to the Sierra del Pinacate, a harsh volcanic field encompassing hundreds of desolate square miles southwest of Organ Pipe Cactus National Monument. Hornaday wrote about his expedition in a remarkable book called *Camp-Fires on Desert and Lava*. The first leg of his journey was between Tucson and Lukeville, or Gringo Pass, as it's come to be called, and he went through Papago Indian country. He wrote:

> . . . they all wore the unattractive remnant of cheap civilization. . . . To me, Anglo-Saxon clothes on a savage invariably look out of place. If an Indian is not picturesque, why is he? During the past twenty years we have had so much thrust upon us about our Southwestern Indians, the whole lot begins to look passe. At present, the only apparent use of the Southwestern Indian is to furnish trips to good fellows who need outings. Ethnologically, he is a squeezed lemon. . . .[3]

This was turn-of-the-century borderland literature. The first of the more recent books about the border, Ovid Demaris's *Poso del Mundo*, published in 1970, was an elaborate guide to whorehouses and corruption. Nonetheless, Demaris recognized the border zone as an entity, the first time this has come across in any major book in the United States.

We get images of the border from movies—Jack Nicholson in *The Border*, Telly Savalas made one, Charles Bronson starred in *Borderline*. Orson Welles made *Touch of Evil*. Even *The Last Picture Show* had a bit of the border in it. In Thalia, up in the Texas Panhandle, Larry McMurtry writes about two high school kids who decide to go to Mexico for the weekend. Sonny and Duane are talking:

> "We could go to Mexico and be back by sometime Monday." The gas station attendant says they shouldn't go: "The water's buggy in Mexico."
> "We'll just drink beer and tequila."
> "I been there. You get the clap and you wish you hadn't drunk nothin'. Where you goin', Laredo?"
> The boys looked at one another. They hadn't planned that far ahead. They were just going to Mexico.
> Duane says, "Let's go all the way to Matamoros, since we're going. I hear it's about the wildest."

> Sam the lion says, "Need any money?"
>
> "No. We got plenty."
>
> "You can't tell," Sam said, fishing out his billfold. "Better take ten dollars for insurance. They say money kinda melts when you take it across the border."[4]

This is the image of the border in a small, Anglo, Texas town. Other books come to mind. *The Rain God*, by Arturo Islas, is a wonderful book of overlapping short stories about a family that lives along the border. It appears to be in the neighborhood of Del Rio, Texas. There is the classic look at South Texas border culture, *"With His Pistol in His Hand*," by Américo Paredes—an entire book devoted to one song, "El Corrido de Gregorio Cortez." A novel by Robert Boswell, *Crooked Hearts*, about intrafamily angst, is set in working-class Yuma.

Mexican movies from the interior skew the border even more than those from the United States. The worse they are, the more successful they become. They portray unbelievable stereotypes of the border of good versus evil, or poor versus poorer; everybody beats everyone else up and everyone has a vicious motive. The movies are pretty nasty. They are also very entertaining. Paralleling that phenomenon are the *novelas*, the little hip-pocket comic books that are, for many, the one form of the printed word. My favorite is a weekly called *Denuncia*. One book is about a couple of Tapachulas in the state of Chiapas. The husband is injured and requires hospitalization, and his wife must come to the United States to earn money. She is smuggled across the border at Tijuana and runs into the requisite problems. Her husband, somewhat mended, comes to the States looking for her and gets pilloried at the border. It's a dramatic saga.

Denuncia has always been my favorite *novela* because it takes actual news events and turns them into comic books. One, published while Anastasio Somoza was still in power in Nicaragua, deals with the feared National Guard; it's called "Massacre in Nicaragua." Another, with a bit of black humor to it, is called "Murdered Reporter."

On to Jack Kerouac, not in *On the Road*, in which he came to Tucson, but in *Lonesome Traveler*, where he walks through the gate at Morely Street into Nogales:

> The moment you cross that little wire gate and you're in Mexico you feel like you just sneaked out of school when you told the teacher you were sick and

she told you you could go home. . . . You walk thirsty through the swinging doors of a saloon and get a bar beer and turn around and there's fellas shooting pool, cooking tacos, wearing sombreros, some wearing guns on their rancher hips and gangs of singing businessmen throwing pesos at the standing musicians who wander up and down the room.—It's a great feeling of entering the Pure Land especially because it's so close to dry faced Arizona and Texas and all over the Southwest—but you can find it, this feeling. . . .[5]

This gets into the beatnik feel for the border in which the most mundane things were incredible. It's true that if you walk into Mexico, you often find Mexicans wearing hats and cooking tacos. No big thing. But Kerouac turned it into the most thrilling event in his life.

Lawrence Ferlinghetti's *The Mexican Night* is a collection that began in 1962 and was published in 1970. This is my one R-rated contribution, a tiny bit scatological. Ferlinghetti is in Baja California. Now picture, if you can, the geography of the Baja Peninsula and how it relates to U.S. California.

Bah on this Baja—who stole the sun? . . . Dig the native habitations, groin streets, mud people. Only the kids and dogs have anything left in them—and the dogs can't stand it. They lie around stretched out with flies all over them in the gutters. . . . Perhaps I could learn to love this land if I stayed a while tho it's the third or fourth time I've been to Mex already—if Los Angeles is the asshole of America, what is this brown appendage down here?[6]

Ferlinghetti takes the bus along the border from Ensenada to Mexicali.

Rode all day, contemplating the earth, saw nothing. Endless riprap of roads, hills, mountains, hopeless houses, trees, sagebrush, fences, dust, burros, dry land . . . passing through Tijuana, I see a legless man at downtown dirt corner sitting in back of antique sedan from which doors have been torn.[7]

Arrived in Mexicali, another dusty town, only worse . . . bus station crammed with campesinos looking grim, tough and hungry, under enormous hats and ponchos, waiting for country buses and revolutions. These are the front teeth of Latin America.[8]

Ferlinghetti crosses into Calexico and back to Mexicali, and he notices some signs posted by the U.S. government. One says you may not reenter the United States with your pet, another says—and this was a real sign—narcotics addicts must register. Ferlinghetti appreciates the anarchy of the border.

"Do not pee on the wrong side of the fence. Show your dog tags. Borders must be maintained!" he wrote, then launched into a lengthy fantasy of a world without borders, in which

> all colors blended into one skin with one tongue. It'll only take 5,000 more years to do this . . . a very simple revolution could accomplish it in no time, declare . . . all national flags into snotrags or bandages to be used in maternity hospitals giving birth to nothing but a new generation of babies of nothing but mixed colors and races.[9]

This is where thinking about the border can lead if you're not careful.

There are a few other books about the border I want to note. One is *Mexican Folk Tales from the Borderlands*, an entertaining collection that began in the first part of this century. And a recent book is Alan Weisman's *La Frontera*, a book that brings insight and wisdom to the border. Undoubtedly there will be more books about the border.

I'll conclude by telling a little story about a Mexican magazine and a story it published about the border. The town of Naco, part of which is in Arizona and part in Sonora, brings chuckles in the interior of Mexico for its name. In slang, it means a rube from the countryside, an easy mark. Not just a buffoon but a dullard. It's used in *telenovelas* broadcast from Mexico City and in hip-pocket *novelas* as well. The magazine editors thought it would be amusing to send a reporter to Naco, Sonora—"those wacky norteños"—and see what they think about the name of their town.

The reporter arrived there and walked around, asking person after person about the town's name. Nobody he ran into knew the meaning of the word, because in Naco, Sonora, they get television from Channel 4 in Tucson. They get the *Arizona Daily Star* and the *Tucson Citizen*. People in the border town of Naco, Sonora, don't get their culture from the interior. The reporter had the feeling that "¡Los de Naco son demaciado naco que no intienden que quiere decir la palabra naco!" ("The people of Naco are so *naco* they don't even know what *naco* means!"). Finally he met a woman who understood exactly what he was doing, indignant that he had come to mock her town. "Just you remember," she scolded him, "¡No somos nacos, sino naquenses!" ("We're not *naco* [stupid], we're Naco citizens!").

Is there a "border literature"? I maintain that there is. It's gotten a bit more sophisticated since William Hornaday's observations about the role of Indians, and I think it illustrates that we *nacos* are headed and writing in the right direction.

NOTES

1. William Carlos Williams, "The Desert Music," in his *Pictures From Brueghel and Other Poems* (New York: New Directions, 1962), 108–116.

2. Graham Greene, *Another Mexico* (New York: Viking Press, 1939), 13.

3. William T. Hornaday, *Camp-Fires on Desert and Lava* (Tucson: University of Arizona Press, 1983), 67.

4. Larry McMurtry, *The Last Picture Show* (New York: New Dial Press, 1966), 126–128.

5. Jack Kerouac, *Lonesome Traveler* (New York: Grove Press, 1960), 21–22.

6. Lawrence Ferlinghetti, *The Mexican Night* (New York: New Directions, 1970), 3–4.

7. Ibid., 7.

8. Ibid., 8.

9. Ibid., 9.

SUGGESTED READINGS

Aiken, Riley. *Mexican Folktales of the Borderland*. Dallas: Southern Methodist University Press, 1980.

Bartlett, John Russell. *Personal Narrative of Explorations and Incidents in Texas, New Mexico, California, Sonora, and Chihuahua Connected with the United States and Mexican Boundary Commission During the Years 1850, '51, '52, and '53*. 2 vols. Chicago: Rio Grande, 1854; repr. 1965.

Boswell, Robert. *Crooked Hearts*. New York: Knopf, 1987.

Demaris, Ovid. *Poso del Mundo*. Boston: Little, Brown, 1970.

Emory, William H. *Report of the United States and Mexican Boundary Survey*. 3 vols. Washington, D.C.: U.S. Department of the Interior, 1857–1859.

Ferlinghetti, Lawrence. *The Mexican Night*. New York: New Directions, 1970. First published 1962.

Greene, Graham. *Another Mexico*. New York: Viking Press, 1939.

Hornaday, William T. *Camp-Fires on Desert and Lava*. Tucson: University of Arizona Press, 1983. First published 1900.

Islas, Arturo. *The Rain God*. Palo Alto, Calif.: Alexandrian Press, 1984.

Kerouac, Jack. *Lonesome Traveler*. New York: Grove Press, 1970.

McMurtry, Larry. *The Last Picture Show*. New York: Dial Press, 1966.

Miller, Tom. *On the Border*. New York: Harper & Row, 1981.

Paredes, Américo. *"With His Pistol in His Hand."* Austin: University of Texas Press, 1973.

Riding, Alan. *Distant Neighbors*. New York: Knopf, 1985.

Weisman, Alan, and Jay Dusard. *La Frontera*. San Diego: Harcourt Brace, Jovanovich, 1986.

Williams, William Carlos. *The Desert Music and Other Poems*. New York: Random House, 1954.

———. *I Wanted to Write a Poem*. New York: Beacon Press, 1958.

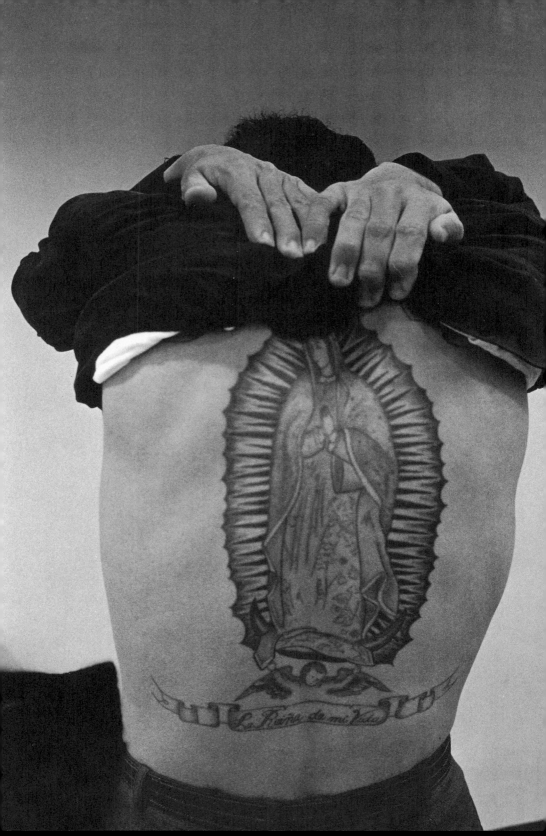

CITY PLACES

La Reina de Mi Vida *(Photograph by Juan Carlos Bernal © 1983)*

PATRICIA PRECIADO MARTIN

Songs My Mother Sang to Me

I want to talk a little about my fiction writing, but I also want you to understand that when I say the word "fiction," I use it very loosely. I don't know exactly what fiction is, and I don't really know if what I am writing now can be called fiction. I think everything that I have written about in my collection of short stories, *Days of Plenty, Days of Want*,[1] is really not fiction to me because all of it has been based on something I experienced either within my own family or within my larger extended family. I use the term "extended family" very loosely, too: all the people I have met and learned to love during the last few years of my work here in Tucson with Mexicano history.[2]

There really hasn't been one story I have ever written where the kernel, the seed, wasn't planted by someone telling me about her or his life, singing the song of her or his history. The *madres, abuelitas, tías,* and *la gente* all have planted the little seed of creativity for me with their *canciones*.

I love being a writer for two reasons. One is that reading is my work. I can live in the life of my mind all the time. And the second reason is that being a writer is like looking through a kaleidoscope. The fact that the picture changes when you rearrange the pieces doesn't make the picture any less true. Every time I give my experiences a little twist in my mind, a new pattern emerges. So in a sense, by being a writer I have been able to be as outrageous a person as I have wanted to be, and no one can say anything.

I also have to be a historian, which I love because I love my culture, my Mexican roots. I can be a detective. I can try to figure things out—

what happened, why things happened—and embellish it. But it doesn't make it any less true. I can also be a romantic, so it's a perfect life.

Let me tell you a story about my grandmother, whom I never met. Her name was Mercedes Rascón Romero, and she was born in the little town of Guerrero in the state of Chihuahua not far from Chihuahua City; she was a mestiza of Tarahumara lineage. She died when my mother was sixteen, and I have a few tiny mementos from her. But they have been so evocative to me that I feel as if I have known this woman, and I have dedicated stories to her. Like Luci Tapahonso, I put the names of real people in my stories.

Listen to this wonderful story. When they were newlyweds, my grandparents moved from Chihuahua to Clifton, Arizona. All their children were born there. My mother used to like to play marbles, something that girls did not do in those days, I guess. It was a boys' game. But my mother was an outdoor type; she liked to play marbles. My grandmother didn't approve that my mother was out there with the boys in the dirt, scuffing her hands. After a great deal of discussion and consideration, my grandmother relented and sewed my mother a little satin pillow with lace all the way around the edges and embroidered her name, Aurelia, on it so that when she played marbles, her hand would never touch the dirt.

What have I done with that story? Well, to me the legacy is this: You can do anything you want as long as your nails are in good condition. I have never felt limited because of my ethnicity or gender.

I have a photograph of my grandmother sitting on a hillside in Clifton. She sewed, my mother told me; she made all their clothes, for they were poor. She is wearing a wonderful gray high-necked blouse with tiny pleats and long sleeves that she had sewn. Her hair is swept up. She is a beautiful woman. She is partly reclining on the hillside with two other women. They must have been out for a picnic. If you look closely at the photograph, my grandmother Mercedes is holding a little bunch of wildflowers in the hand resting in her lap. And that tells me so much about her. Her appreciation of nature, her love for the delicate, her appreciation of beauty and the unexpected. So in a sense, without ever having known her, I can feel her presence.

My mother tells another story, a sad story. When my grandmother died, it was of a broken heart. Now I know there is a story in that, but I haven't written it yet. My mother was only sixteen years old and had to assume the responsibility of raising her younger brothers and sisters. It was a very difficult life for her. And she was so upset when my grandmother died that she took all the saints off their home altar and put them upside down in a drawer and shut that drawer for years. I love that story because it teaches me that when the going gets rough, you can't even depend on the Guy up there. You've got to do it on your own. And in a sense that's what I mean about historical legacy.

One of the very interesting images that I always get when I talk to people is an imagery of our culture in terms of food. It is very well known that so much that is evocative is your memory of food cooking; the sense of smell is a powerful trigger. I know that is true for me. I can close my eyes and see myself in my mother's kitchen, walking in that door after school and looking in the pot.

There is nothing quite like making tortillas in terms of Mexican American culture. It isn't the food in and of itself, obviously, but what is associated with food. My mother always talked about the fact that from the time she was five years old, she was responsible for all the tortillas in her family of eleven. She was so small that my grandmother gave her a box to stand on so she could reach the kitchen counter to make tortillas every day. Now here is where the interesting imagery comes in. She didn't talk about a stack of tortillas, a bunch of tortillas, a pile of tortillas. You know how my mother described it? *Un altar de tortillas.* An altar of tortillas my mother made! If I were the pope, I wouldn't have that Virgen de Guadalupe just standing doing nothing. I would have the Virgen de Guadalupe standing at an altar decorated not with roses but with tortillas.

This tradition about the tortillas has been a real problem for me because I have never really learned to make tortillas. Once I made them right, but it is not easy. I think about my children, for my mother is no longer alive, but they remember. My father made two little *palotes* (rolling pins), one for each of my kids. Whenever they went to my mother's, they would make tortillas. And of course I have my mother's *palote* that I make tortillas with, but it doesn't help. Of all the few little treasures I have of mother, that is the thing I value the most. So I wrote an article about my mother and tortilla-making. I'll share a little bit from it with you.

If life is a bowl of albondigas, what am I doing getting skimmed off the top?

There are a few things that I must first explain about my mother. She has an inborn elegance and grace; a genetic exquisiteness. People turn their head when she walks by.

I have spent most of my life walking a few paces behind her, pretending to carry the train of an imagined magnificent gossamer cape. She is regal. And there is no place where she reigns more absolutely than in her "kingdom of the Kitchen." There she has decreed irrevocable laws with monarchical absoluteness. There she is the queen, and I, alas, the court jester.

The laws of the kitchen are as follows:

Law No. 1: Tamales are not made; they are sculpted.

Law No. 2: Sopa is not soup—it is "The Lovely Broth."

Law No. 3: One must always wear an apron when embarking on a "Kitchen Mission." The apron must be handmade and embroidered with the day of the week, preferably in cross-stitch, and the correct one worn each day.

Law No. 4: A table must always have a starched and ironed cloth—never, never place mats.

Law No. 5: Tortillas are the essence of life, the symbol of eternity, the circle that is unbroken, the shortest distance between two points.

Law No. 6: Law No. 5 takes precedence over laws one through four and the Six Precepts of the Roman Catholic Church.

People who buy their tortillas from the market wrapped in plastic might as well move to Los Angeles, for they have already lost their souls.

And Mom tries to teach me. She never did. I said, "Well, Mom, how much flour?" "Well, mihijita" (she gestured with hands to indicate amount). "Well, how much salt?" "Well, mihijita" (again gesturing with fingers to indicate amount).

Last week my sister came over, and we went through the whole thing. She said, "Well, I don't know. This is about right—of course, this not the size of the bowl that Mom had. Why didn't we measure?" But it was impossible. I'd always go over to Mother's and she would try to teach me how to make tortillas. It never worked.

Mother would say, "Measure? Who needs to measure? You feel if the amount is all right. Your heart will tell you. See? I cup my hand like this and I know it has enough baking powder. The flour? Just make a lovely little mound of it like this in the center of the bowl, just a pinch of salt in the water. You can tell when you have put enough. The Virgin of Guadalupe will guide you."

I have already broken one of her favorite cups during one of our morning coffee sessions. There is part of a scrambled egg glowing on her clean table cloth and she told me three times to lower my voice and put on an apron—the one that says Martes (Tuesday). She always has a candle burning for me in front of her homemade altar—unspecified intentions, but I think it has something to do with the fact that I use place mats and paper napkins.

Well, I try. I take the palote and try to roll the dough out into circles. The dough has a life of its own. It resists, gathers strength, overpowers and subdues me.

My mother says, "That one doesn't look too bad mihijita. It's not quite round, that's true, but let's cook it and see how it comes out."

And she places my tortilla on the comal. It energizes with the heat. It browns, it puffs, it multiplies. It grows appendages, it hardens. The morning progresses. My stack of tortillas grows at a precarious tilt, a leaning Tower of Babel. I am exhausted.

Mother says, "Mihija, now we're done. That was easy. They look better than the last time. Children, come and see the tortillas your mother has made!"

And then my children: "Your tortillas look funny, Mom. How come they don't look like Nani's? That one looks like a rabbit. That one looks like a mushroom. That one looks like Africa. And that one looks like Texas." It wouldn't have been so bad, I suppose, if one of them had been shaped like the state of Jalisco—but Texas is unacceptable. Mamacita relights the candle to St. Jude, the patron of hopeless cases.[3]

There is a lot here besides the misshapen tortillas in terms of community, in terms of love, in terms of family. In terms of a support system, in terms of power, in terms of connection and legacy.

This is going to sound funny, but I worry. Do you know that very few people my age make tortillas? I make them, but they are crooked. Mine is the last generation, I think, to make tortillas.

But I would also like to mention that in my short stories there are men who are powerful. But when the men are involved, the power in my stories is, in a sense, the feminine side of the men. The romantic, spiritual, sensitive, beauty-oriented side of a man that we in our society call the feminine side.

Such a man is Don Federico Sotomayor, the old vegetable vendor, who polishes the old silver bridle every night by lamplight in his little shack. He inherited it from he doesn't know whom. It has been passed down. So Don Federico polishes his bridle and admires it, and reminisces about his past and thinks about his future. And so is the little cowboy, Alfredo, in *The Legend of the Bellringer of San Agustin*, who knows the secret of the bell. He is also very sensitive, very beauty-oriented. Open spaces in the mind.

One of my stories, which was based on my mother, is called "María de las Trenzas, Mary of the Braids." In one way I am trying to make an important point I would like to share with you. It is the story of a young woman who has stayed home to take care of her widowed father. All her sisters and brothers have left, are married, and have families of their own. But she, out of a sense of obligation, becomes a surrogate wife to her aging, widowed father. She is culturally bound by obligation, as was my mother, who did not have a life of her own. She sublimated all her needs, all her desires, and all her dreams so that she could serve her father. And so her life became the life of her mind, in her fantasies, and so "María de las Trenzas" is a story about a young woman who every day goes through the motions of cooking *las tortillas* and cleaning and mending—all those things. But in her mind she lives another life.

The important point of my story is that if you are ethnocentric to the point of not choosing what is good and rejecting what is not good, you are harming yourself. What happened to María de las Trenzas is that she incorporated into herself some of the aspects of our culture that were not good for her and limited her.

Yet that is what the beauty of biculturalism is. We can, as Luci Tapahonso says, live in two cultures. What you do is choose the most positive and the most powerful, the most evocative and the most spiritually meaningful things from both.

So María de las Trenzas struggled with her desire for a life of her own and her feeling of obligation to her father. Her friends leave after a visit.

María accompanies them to the front door to say adiós and returns to her chair and the basket of mending in the kitchen. She threads a needle and with her head bent and braids cascading over her shoulders, she sews a button on her father's Sunday shirt. She hunches her shoulders wearily as the day looms before her. The weight of her duties is like the weight of her braids, more mending and sewing, washing and folding, scrubbing and dusting, sweeping and mopping, errand-running and cooking and the evening stupor of her father's absorbed silence rising to the ceiling like the smoke from his pipe. The only voice is the one droning from the black and white TV. The only conversation, the one between her father's creaking chair and the crickets that have escaped the scrutiny of her broom. Her only true companions, the well-thumbed books that whisper their secrets to her during the long evenings in her room. Today is like yesterday and tomorrow. All her days connected and identical, like the dolls she cut from folded paper as a child. María brushes back her heavy braids absentmindedly. She removes newly sharpened scissors from the sewing basket and concentrating, she deftly trims and snips fabric for the patch in her father's overalls. Her brow furrows in thought. There are no distractions now. Only the warbling of the imprisoned canary, Julio, and the ticking of the clock in the living room. It chimes two o'clock.

Then her father, Don Antonio Castillo, wipes his shoes carefully on the door-mat and enters the house. He calls to María in greeting, but there is no reply. An emptiness almost palatable looms in the sala, the living room. He calls again. "María!" Silence. No cooking odors waft from the stove. Supper will be late. He goes into the kitchen, a scolding on his lips. The stove is cold. The frying pans empty. The cage door of Julio, the canary, is ajar, the canary nowhere in sight. Don Antonio turns around, puzzlement on his face, and then he sees coiled on the table by the window the two long and luxurious braids that María has cut neatly from the nape of her neck.[4]

One of the things that concerns me now, and I try to deal with it in my writing, is open spaces and city places in a symbolic sense, in a sense of change. In the sense I ask myself, Are we losing what we have, and does it concern me? Just in the last few years, I have seen so many changes in Tucson that are important to us as Mexicanos. We are becoming a homogenized culture, and I think that a lot of the beauty of our community is the variety. In a sense I try to deal with that.

In two more of my stories, "Tierra a Tierra" and "Las Ruinas," I also try to deal with the idea of culture. One of the stories was based on a real experience that stayed with me for several years before I did anything with it. I had been told about María, an elderly woman in a nursing home. When I went to interview her, she had deteriorated to the point where we couldn't have much conversation in terms of her memories. But she was very eager to visit her little house. She had lived in a little adobe house in the cluster of adobe houses at the foot of "A" Mountain along the river. So I made arrangements with the people from the nursing home to take her to her *casita*. They insisted on coming because she was fairly frail. We took one of the vans and went there.

María's house had been empty for many months. Some of the windows had been broken, but the doors were intact. All over that house, stuck to the windows and to the walls and in the drawers and on the mirrors, were little notes that she had written to herself, as if she was trying to remind herself of her own existence or give herself context. If she said a rosary that day, she'd write it down. If she went to the store and got something, she'd put the date, "went to the store today and got this and that." Or she would think about something in her family and would write it down. There were literally thousands of little scraps of paper stuck to every possible surface.

It was the oddest experience I have ever had. But that idea stayed with me, and I kept thinking there had to be a story in that. And there was. In "The Ruins, La Ruinas," there is a young teenaged girl, Alma, who is kind of a misfit at school. Her mother is extremely religious, spending a great deal of her time at church. And her father is an intellectual. She is a loner. Quite by accident Alma discovers an old ruin by the river and a very ancient and mysterious woman living there. She befriends the old woman, who is so ancient that you couldn't guess her age. She has been the keeper of the culture, and has written down all the history of the Mexicano people in the Tucson area on tiny scraps of paper. In a sense, that is what I saw in Doña María's home. In other words, only *she* could give herself reality, I think, in her isolated life in the barrio. She knew she was real only because she wrote it down that she was real. I used that imagery in this story, applying it to a woman I called Doña Luz (Light), who is the keeper of the culture and on her tiny slips of paper has written all the important history of the Mexican people. I am concerned about our legacy. I feel that it is very, very fragile, and I don't know what is going to happen. I don't know if it will be saved or not. So I'm going to close with a very short excerpt.

On this visit by Alma to the little old lady in the ruins, it happens to be one of those rare days in Tucson when it snows. Doña Luz leads Alma to the ruin, and there Alma sees all the tattered scraps of paper. At first she thinks they are moths. Doña Luz explains that this is the history of the people that she has gathered and written, and Alma reads from many of the tattered little scraps. Doña Luz writes about the transfer of land. She writes about the history of different people. She writes down prayers. She writes about the traditions of the fiestas. She writes down all the things that she is afraid will be lost. While Alma is reading the last strip of paper, the snowstorm is building and the wind is blowing, and the storm becomes more severe. She begins to read one of the last scraps of paper.

The unfinished song flew from Alma's hand when suddenly and without warning a tornado-like gust blew open the unlocked door of Doña Luz's hovel. The airborne flakes blasted in with a ferociousness and Alma saw helpless and aghast that the shreds of precious paper in an avalanche of blinding whiteness had metamorphosed into giant white moths. They quickened with life and took to the air with a dizzying funnel of flight, blowing snow mingled with blowing paper and rose and fell and rose and fell and then eddied into a blizzard of memories. And then the memories and the spirit of Doña Luz fluttered out the open door in a thousand flowing fragments in the direction of the south wind somewhere west of Atzlan.[5]

NOTES

1. Patricia Preciado Martin, *Days of Plenty, Days of Want* (Tempe: Hispanic Research Center, Arizona State University, Bilingual Press/Review, 1989).

2. I have been working as a field historian for the Arizona Historical Society in the Mexican Heritage Project since 1982. The project was funded by local grants and by a grant from the National Endowment for the Humanities. It resulted in a two-year research project on the history of Tucson's Mexican American community from the Gadsen Purchase to World War II. The result was Thomas Sheridan's *Los Tucsonenses* (Tucson: University of Arizona Press, 1986). The Mexican Heritage Project collected thousands of photographs, dozens of oral histories, and other artifacts. It also has reinstituted the Fiesta de San Agustín, Tucson's oldest traditional fiesta. Each year since 1983, a different exhibit has been put up in conjunction with the celebration of the fiesta.

3. Patricia Preciado Martin, "Bridging the Tortilla Generation Gap," *Arizona Daily Star*, May 1979.

4. Patricia Preciado Martin, "María de las Trenzas," in *Days of Plenty, Days of Want*, 47–48.

5. Patricia Preciado Martin, "The Ruins," in *Days of Plenty, Days of Want*, 20.

LAWRENCE CLARK POWELL

Who? When? Where?

What do I mean by this volley of "w" words: who, when, and where? Those words are journalese—lead questions meant to be answered by reporters. My intention is to apply them to literature, which is what every conference such as this should regard as its end product. Literature should be the lasting residue of both group and individual effort.

I am interested only in prose or poetry that rises above journalese because it has that mysterious additional life which it imparts to its readers. All other writing passes away, or stands and waits as a reference book, and thus makes work for librarians. Nothing wrong about that, says this former librarian.

I know what Doctor Johnson said about the person who writes for anything but money. Yet even as he said it, he must have known that his lexicographical drudgery would outlast all the king's gold. There has always been a time in which more writers starved than grew fat. As a writer throughout my other life, I never felt that anybody owed me anything as a writer. There *are* ways a writer can make a living other than writing. Few of us ever hit the jackpot, or ever will. Lucky us.

What were some of a writer's survival routes before the age of fellowships, grants, workshops, conferences, and so-called creative writing courses? Melville served on the docks, Emerson lectured, Eliot worked in a bank, Auden worked the campuses, Forster was a college don, peripatetic Thomas read his poetry and drank other men's booze, Larkin was a librarian who would have been poet laureate if he had not chosen not to be.

Does it sound like I disapprove of creative writing courses? Only of using the word "creative." Good basic writing can and should be taught. Carpenter work can't be taught too early. Creativity can't ever be taught because we don't know what it is.

What do I mean by "creativity"? It is that mysterious art of conceiving and arranging language that lives in every word, sentence, paragraph, and page, so that its writer is unmistakable from the first. Such a writer has the birthright gift of the three "S's": the power to see, to sense, to say—that is, of sight, feeling, and expression. There are never many writers so endowed alive at any given time. They tend to appear in clusters and to sustain each other and give their names to an age—the Athens of Pericles, the Elizabethan age, the flowering of New England.

I believe what Cyril Connolly says about writing in *The Unquiet Grave*. He starts right out in overdrive.

> The more books we read, the sooner we perceive that the only function of a writer is to produce a masterpiece. No other task is of any consequence. Obvious though this should be, how few writers will admit it, or having made the admission, will be prepared to lay aside the piece of iridescent mediocrity on which they have embarked. Writers always hope that their next book will be their best, for they will not acknowledge that it is their present way of life which prevents them from ever creating anything different or better.[1]

Elsewhere Connolly named what he called the Enemies of Promise. I haven't reread his book of that title since it first appeared in 1938, yet I do remember that his greatest of all the enemies is success.

"Success," Trollope wrote, "is a poison to be taken only late in life, and then in small doses." Of course those of you who are writers won't believe that. I didn't either, until I arrived at what is called "late in life," and wondered if I had been overlooked. In our time, success has been hoisted to celebrity level whose firepower is the blockbuster, which follows the million-dollar advance. I shall ignore those living writers whose books are bought and sold by weight.

Literary celebrity reared its ugly head in our time (my time, the year 1929) with Oliver La Farge's first and best novel, *Laughing Boy*. It won the Pulitzer Prize and, as its author later observed, hung round his neck the rest of his life like the albatross. Name your own succeeding celebrities: Sinclair Lewis, Pearl Buck, Hemingway, Fitzgerald, Thomas Wolfe, Salinger, Steinbeck—all victims of too much, too early.

Few writers can reject the embrace of the harlot Celebrity. Let me introduce supporting data from the last century about one who could. Melville was perhaps the first to say no to Celebrity. He stands like a lighthouse to warn of the rocks beneath the surface. Every few years I go back to those exalted letters he wrote to his neighbor Hawthorne in the midst of writing *Moby Dick*, that book in which he took a last deep-sea dive.

Melville had to leave town in order to write *Moby Dick*. He quit Manhattan for the family's country house in the Berkshires, a stately old place called Arrowhead. High in his crow's-nest study, with a view north to Graylock, he wrote that great novel—and to save his life. Save his soul he did, yet at the same time he lost his reputation with the reading public.

Melville's first book made him into what was then a celebrity. It was the South Sea idyll *Typee*. Public and publisher clamored for more of the same. Melville tried to give it to them in *Omoo, Mardi, Redburn,* and *White Jacket*. All of them were based on more of his whaling ship adventures. He added an ingredient, however, that the public did *not* want: philosophy. What they wanted was more of that South Sea maiden Fayaway. His public demanded *Typee II, Typee III*, ad nauseam, even as nearly a century later La Farge's public and publisher called for *Laughing Boy II*.

Melville tried to please the public and at the same time to be the self he had discovered himself to be. He left the Madison Avenue of his time, buried himself in the Berkshires, and sweated out *Moby Dick*. Not only would he give them what they wanted, he would give them what they ought to have. He gave them "the works," in which he unloaded everything he knew about whales, oceans, ships, men, and life, all in one whale of a book. His was the most costly creative act in our literature, the only one to stand with *Leaves of Grass*. Melville paid for that book with his own genius. It could never be used in a creative writing class, for it is a bad novel and a great book, one never to be copied.

It was in the course of creating *Moby Dick*, and in the afterglow, that Melville wrote those heart-shaking letters to Hawthorne.

My dear sir, they begin to patronize. All Fame is patronage. Let me be infamous. There is no patronage in *that*. What reputation H.M. has is horrible. Think of it! To go down to posterity is bad enough, anyway; but to go down

to it as a man who lived among cannibals! *Typee* will be given to babies, perhaps, with their gingerbread. I have come to regard this matter of Fame as
the most transparent of all vanities.[2]

That letter was written in June 1851, a month before *Moby Dick*
was published. Whereupon Melville exulted to Hawthorne, "I have
written a wicked book, and feel spotless as the lamb."

I confess to mixed feelings about Hawthorne. Charges can be brought
against him for his preoccupation with his own work, to the neglect
of that of his fellow writers. Hawthorne was a cold fish, no whale, no
mammal. Yet to his everlasting glory, he did not fail to respond to Melville's book. What would we not give for the letter he wrote to acknowledge *Moby Dick*, a letter long lost and of which we know only from
Melville's response to it as a "joy-giving and exultation-breeding letter,"
and continuing in this almost delirious vein, ". . . a sense of unspeakable
security is in me this moment, on account of your having understood
the book."[3]

For lack of another Hawthorne, Melville's genius withered and died.
He turned his back on public and publisher, and for eighteen years he
worked as a customs inspector on the Manhattan docks. Yet he kept the
flame alive though burning low. Henceforth he wrote only for himself,
his family, and a few friends, while his masterpiece sank into limbo until resurrected in 1910 by the first biography, Raymond Weaver's
Melville: Mariner and Mystic. *Moby Dick* has never stopped living the
long life of constant readership.

I have elaborated about the *who* and the *where*. What about the
when? If too much early success often proves fatal, when *should* it
come? It is best not early nor late nor too much in a single dose, but
rather over an extended period, thus sparing the writer the devastating
attendants.

In prose, which he rarely wrote, Robinson Jeffers had things to say
about fame and when it best comes: "But a young man writes, 'What
good will it do me to imagine myself remembered after death? If I am to
have fame and an audience, I want them now while I can feel them.'"
Jeffers went on to say:

It seems to me that the young man speaks in ignorance. To be peered at and
interviewed, to be pursued by idlers and autograph seekers and inquiring ad-

mirers, would surely be a sad nuisance. And it is destructive too, if you take it seriously, it wastes your energy into self-consciousness; it destroys spontaneity and soils the springs of the mind. Whereas posthumous recognition could do you no harm at all, and is really the only kind worth considering.[4]

Although I have not included living writers, I intend to make one exception. He is the only writer among us to whom I yield as my senior in age, talent, and wisdom. He is Frank Waters, who personifies for me much of what I have been saying about who, when, and where. If he has at times left the mountains and desert of his birth and long life, it has been to go south to Mexico, not east to Manhattan. Frank Waters never came west; he was already here, from birth in the Colorado Rockies. He winters now in Tucson, because the snows of northern New Mexico require shovel more than typewriter.

Although he would agree that he could have used the money that comes with celebrity, he has been fortunate not to have been buried alive under a blockbuster. His prime time was a quieter one, when a writer still had charge of his own destiny.

In the foreword to Terence Tanner's bibliography, Waters is perceptive and honest in looking back at fifty years of his writing. None of his books was initially successful beyond a modest sale. When they were published east of the Hudson and drew favorable reviews, they were nevertheless still allowed to go out of print. Waters's words from his bibliography are relevant:

> Every writer, whether he admits it or not, hankers after fame and fortune. That I did not attain them was the best thing that ever happened to me. I was compelled to keep following the carrot dangling before my nose by doing still another book.[5]

To a remarkable one-man publisher, Alan Swallow, Waters owed his survival and resurrection. When Swallow had faith in a book, he kept it in print. Such were *The Man Who Killed the Deer* and *People of the Valley*. They remain high among the literature about the Indians and Hispanics of the Southwest, even as his *The Colorado* is at the peak of books about the West's greatest river before it was doomed and dammed.

Waters endeared himself to me as man as well as writer when he sided with me in a disagreement with Alan Swallow when I was asked to write a foreword to the Northland Press edition of *The Man Who Killed the Deer*. I said that the *where* of the book was more important than the *what*; that is, the Taos setting outweighed the mystical philosophy. I saw the land as more important than theories about its dwellers. I still feel that way. Swallow didn't. When we appealed to Frank, he said that inasmuch as the foreword was by Powell and not Swallow, it should be left as Larry wrote it. And it was.

I have been reading D. H. Lawrence's collected letters. Volume 4 covers the years 1921–1924, during which Lawrence came for the first time to northern New Mexico. It struck me how much alike his and Waters's visions are of that land. Similar also is the way both writers rejected celebrity. After the English years of poverty, censorship, and rejection, Lawrence's books were at last selling—in America, not England. Even so, he refused to be lionized. When asked to come to New York and lecture (the time's equivalent of TV talk shows), he refused. He said he didn't want to be seen in the company of Hugh Walpole and his countrymen who were milking the American cow for all she would give.

Lawrence reached America via Ceylon, Australia, and California. After two weeks near Perth, he and Frieda settled for two months in a seacoast village forty miles south of Sydney. From there he wrote to his sister-in-law, "We live mostly with the sea—not much with the land—and not at all with the people. We don't know a soul on this side of the continent. I have letters of invitation and do not intend to present them."[6] Even so, he read the Sydney newspapers and met a politician and a labor leader, and before the two months were over, he had written *Kangaroo*, which many say is still one of the best of all Australian novels. And quite simply because it has the three S's.

Both Lawrence and Waters insisted that their publishers respect their rights, creative and financial. They were professional writers of the highest integrity who were spared celebrity.

If one is to write literature—that is, prose which endures—the *where* is perhaps the most important of the "w" words. Such are the river of *Huck Finn*, the ocean of *Moby Dick*, the Big Sur coast of Jeffers, the Southwest of *Laughing Boy*, *The Man Who Killed the Deer*, and *People of the Valley*, clear back to the wine-dark sea and Ithaca of the *Odyssey*.

In all of them the *where* is what is lasting—not the fashions, politics, manners, trends, all the changing ephemera of humanity but, rather, the eternal emotions of love and hunger, of survival through war, famine, and pestilence, played out in the natural setting. These give lasting life to literature.

NOTES

1. Cyril Connolly, *The Unquiet Grave* (London: Horizon, 1944), 1.

2. Herman Melville, *Representative Selections*, W. Thorpe, ed. (New York: American Book Co., 1938), 392.

3. Ibid.

4. Robinson Jeffers, *Poetry, Gongorism, and a Thousand Years* (Los Angeles: Ward Ritchie Press, 1949), 11–12.

5. Terence Tanner, *Frank Waters* (Glenwood, Ill.: Meyerbooks, 1983), x.

6. D. H. Lawrence, *Letters*, vol. 4 (Cambridge: Cambridge University Press, 1987), 262.

C. L. SONNICHSEN

Partnerships: A Sort of Conclusion

Some questions were raised by the title of the Southwestern literature conference from which the essays in this book were drawn, "Open Spaces, City Places." It seemed to imply that the two were worlds apart—as if we had to choose between them. It seemed to be saying that the city is the city and the country is the country, and never the twain shall meet. Isn't there a close relationship between the two, especially in the western states? Could one exist without the other?

The idea that cities have played a major role in the development of the western states has had new emphasis in our time. In days gone by, we liked to think of the West as open country, virgin land, a place of sun and solitude where a few rugged settlers battled blizzards and bandits and conquered the wilderness with little help from anybody. The country was open, sparsely settled, and unspoiled. The settlers were there because they liked elbow room and independence. City life was not for them.

City people, on the other hand, preferred to live close to other people with the blessings of civilization—whatever that meant—close at hand. They wanted schools and supermarkets, concerts and conventions, sidewalks and sanitation. They might take short vacations in the open spaces, but their spirits would wither if they had to live there. They perceived a great gulf between the city and the country, and they preferred it that way.

Since 1959, however, when Richard C. Wade published *The Urban West*, we have learned to take a different view of the West and its people. We perceive a new relationship between city places and open spaces, and we can begin to accept Wade's idea that western history is largely urban history.

The word "urban" is a bit troublesome because it means "city," and although we know that the West has some fabulous cities, we also know that the urban West occupies a very small fraction of the western area. We begin to understand better, however, when we note that most of the people have always lived in population centers and only a small percentage have settled in the open spaces. Even this small percentage has been much reduced by the movement, especially during and after World War II, of the rural population to the urban centers. The most important argument, however, is that the towns came before settlement was possible. The town was the hub of the wheel; the settlers were the spokes, radiating out into the surrounding country.

In the beginning there were few cities, but every frontier hamlet was ambitious to become one. They often betrayed their ambitions by addition of the word "city" to their names—Colorado City, Tuba City, Mowry City. Only a few of them made it. Tucson, only a mud village in 1849 when the Forty-niners came charging through, became a metropolis, but no trace remains of places like Estey City in the Tularosa country of New Mexico. The towns that did not become cities, however, were essential to the settlement of the country and qualified as urban centers—hubs of their local wheels—making settlement possible. It would probably be better to call the hub a community, a word with two-way stretch covering all sizes and shapes, from Arizona's Punkin Center to Phoenix.

To bring this idea into visual range, look for a moment at a typical picture: a lone rider moving through an enormous western landscape, a vast level plain with purple mountains far away on the horizon, no human habitation in sight, no traveled road, only the dim trail underfoot and the blue and boundless sky overhead. "Ah," you say, "the great open spaces, untrammeled and unpolluted. The lonely human being, undismayed by solitude, living in harmony with nature, equal to the challenge of the wilderness, the essential man we have all, at one time or another, wished to be. What a contrast with the wage slave living by the clock in the city!"

Well, think again! The man, you will note, is in motion. He is going somewhere—probably heading for a community, without which he would perish in his magnificent isolation. He is heading for a hotel where he can get a bath and a meal, a store where he can replenish his supplies, a saloon where he can relax and find fellowship, a doctor if he gets shot in the saloon, and a Boot Hill where the undertaker can bury him. If he survives, he can head back to his ranch or his mining claim, refreshed and renewed. He would be lost forever without the community.

On the other hand, the community needs him as much as he needs the community. It is there to supply his needs and help him realize some, at least, of his dreams. Without him the community would not exist.

The relationship changes, of course, as the community grows and the country is settled, but the interdependence is still there and will never change. City places and open spaces can't be divorced, even though they exist separately and are, in their way, different worlds.

Larry McMurtry was heading in this direction when he remarked in *In a Narrow Grave* that the history of his native Texas is largely urban history. He would have cleared up some confusion if he had said "community history," but his argument would have been the same.

Man, as we all know, is a gregarious animal, and our history is the history of people in groups. Our fiction, likewise, is about people interacting with each other. It would be hard to make a novel about a hermit with no human contacts. To deal with him at all, it would be necessary to retrace his steps and find out why he could not get along with his fellow men and had to leave the pack.

At the same time we are all individuals living in our own private wildernesses. What we are all looking for is a bridge between the one and the many.

The essayists in this collection are building these bridges for us—showing the connections between men and nature, men and men, men and women. What else, really, is there to talk about?

NOTES ON CONTRIBUTORS

RUDOLFO ANAYA

is professor of English at the University of New Mexico. He is the author of *Bless Me, Ultima* and many fiction titles, including *Alburquerque* (1992).

CHARLES BOWDEN

is a native Tucsonan and works as a free-lance writer. He is the author of many books, including *Blue Desert* (University of Arizona Press, 1986) and *Frog Mountain Blues* (with photographs by Jack W. Dykinga, University of Arizona Press, 1987). His most recent books are *The Secret Forest* (1993) and *Trust Me: Charlie Keating and the Missing Billion* (with Michael Binstein, 1993).

DON GRAHAM

is J. Frank Dobie Regents Professor of American and English literature at the University of Texas in Austin, where he teaches courses in Southwestern and American literature. He is the author of numerous books, including *No Name on the Bullet: A Biography of Audie Murphy* (1989) and *Cowboys and Cadillacs* (1983). He is currently at work on a travel book about France.

ROLANDO HINOJOSA-SMITH

is the Ellen Clayton Garwood Professor in the Department of English at the University of Texas. His *Klail City Death Trip Series* is a multi-volume novel, parts of which have appeared in Dutch, English, French, German, and Spanish. His latest publications are *Korean Love Songs/Korea Liebes Lieder*, a German-English bilingual edition (1991), and *The Useless Servants*.

PATRICIA PRECIADO MARTIN

is a native Arizonan and lifelong Tucsonense who has been active in many facets of the Chicano community, including being a consultant to the Mexican Heritage Project at the Arizona Historical Society for over a decade. She has published four books: *The Legend of the Bellringer of San Agustin* (1979), a bilingual children's story; *Days of Plenty, Days of Want* (1988), a collection of prize-winning short stories; and two collections of oral history of the Mexican American people in Arizona: *Images and Conversations* (1983) and *Songs My Mother Sang to Me* (1992), both published by the University of Arizona Press. She reads and lectures widely on her work.

LEO MARX

is professor of American cultural history (emeritus) at M.I.T. He teaches in the Program in Science, Technology, and Society. He is the author of *The Pilot and the Passenger* (1988) and coeditor (with Susan Daily) of *The Railroad in American Art* (1988), as well as *The Machine in the Garden* (1964).

TOM MILLER

has written six books, including *Trading with the Enemy: A Yankee Travels Through Castro's Cuba* (1992), *The Panama Hat Trail* (1986), and the classic *On the Border: Portraits of America's Southwestern Frontier* (University of Arizona Press, 1985). He has taught writing to students from grade school through university level, and has given talks about borderland literature in the United States and Mexico.

LAWRENCE CLARK POWELL,

a librarian emeritus of the University of California, Los Angeles, currently lives in Tucson. A well-known bibliophile, he served as book review editor of *Westways* and founded the literary journal *Books of the Southwest*. He is the author of *Southwest Classics: The Creative Literature of the Arid Lands—Essays on the Books and Their Writers* (University of Arizona Press, 1974) and *Books Are Basic: The Essential Lawrence Clark Powell*, edited by John David Marshall (University of Arizona Press, 1985).

C. L. SONNICHSEN

began his teaching career at the Texas College of Mines (now University of Texas at El Paso) and retired forty-one years later in 1972, having served as chairman of the English Department and as dean of the Graduate School. He is the author of twenty-six books on topics from histories to humor in Western fiction. His works include *Billy King's Tombstone* (1942), *Ten Texas Feuds* (1957), *The Laughing West* (1988), and *Texas Humoresque* (1990). He died at his Tucson home in 1991.

LUCI TAPAHONSO

is an assistant professor of English at the University of Kansas in Lawrence, where she teaches courses in poetry writing, modern American poetry, and Native American literature. She is the author of four books of poetry, including *Sáanii Dahataał, The Women Are Singing: Poems and Stories* (University of Arizona Press, 1993). Professor Tapahonso was born in Shiprock, New Mexico, and is a member of the Navajo Nation.

JUDY NOLTE TEMPLE

(formerly Judy Nolte Lensink) is associate professor of English and women's studies at the University of Arizona. She directed the 1985 and the 1987 Writers of the Purple Sage conferences from which this book and an earlier volume, *Old Southwest/New Southwest*, evolved. She also has written *"A Secret to Be Buried": The Diary and Life of Emily*

Hawley Gillespie, 1858–1888. Currently she is doing research on the private writings of Colorado's infamous Baby Doe Tabor.

FREDERICK TURNER

is author of six books of nonfiction, among them *Beyond Geography, Rediscovering America, Spirit of Place,* and *A Border of Blue.* His essays have appeared in the *New York Times, Los Angeles Times, International Herald Tribune, American Heritage,* and *Smithsonian.*

STEWART L. UDALL

is an Arizona native who served as secretary of the interior for eight years during the administrations of Presidents Kennedy and Johnson. He is the author of several books, including *The Quiet Crisis* (1963), *1976: Agenda for Tomorrow* (1968), and *To the Inland Empire: Coronado and Our Spanish Legacy* (1987). Mr. Udall now lives in Santa Fe, New Mexico, where he writes and serves as chairman of the board of the Archaeological Conservancy.

PETER WILD

is a professor of English at the University of Arizona. He recently edited the autobiography of John C. Van Dyke, found in the attic of an old farmhouse in Cranbury, New Jersey. The book was published in 1993 by the University of Utah Press.

ANN ZWINGER

is a natural history writer and illustrator living in Colorado Springs. She is the author of some dozen books, mostly on the West and Southwest, including *Run, River, Run* (1975), which won the John Burroughs Award, *Desert Country Near the Sea* (1984), and *Wind in the Rock* (1978). On occasion she teaches nature writing at Colorado College.